# *The way of*
# THE LEOPARD

## *Gillian van Houten*

SPEARHEAD

Published by Spearhead
An imprint of New Africa Books (Pty) Ltd
99 Garfield Road
Claremont
South Africa

(021) 674 4136
info@newafricabooks.co.za

Data and photographs gathered by the team of:
Graham Cookes
Elmon Mhlongo
Karin Slater
Gillian van Houten
John Varty
John Varty led the project.

First edition, first impression 2003

ISBN: 0-86486-559-7
Editing by Sue Ollerhead
Layout and design by Fresh Identity
Cover design by Fresh Identity
Origination by House of Colours
Printing and binding by ABC Press, Cape Town

# CONTENTS

# DEDICATION

To the Mother Leopard, the Pathfinder

This story has its origins in the life of a leopard that lived at Londolozi Game Reserve in South Africa some years ago. Mother Leopard, as she came to be known, is dead now, but she remains a living legend in these parts. It was she who opened the way for leopards at Londolozi.

When we first came to know her, she was shy and elusive. With time trust grew and she shared more and more of her life with us.

During the 15 or so years she lived at Londolozi, she touched our lives in such pivotal and transforming ways that her influence continues until today, resonating like ripples across a pond after some deep disturbance within.

The events of this story about Little Boy and Little Girl Leopard, are part of the legacy she left.

These are only hints and guesses.

Hints followed by guesses; and the rest is prayer,

observance, discipline, thought and action.

T.S. Eliot: *The Dry Salvages (Four Quartets)*

# FOREWORD

This is not a wildlife study, not in the traditional sense. It is an exploration of an experience with wildlife, an encounter. It is what author Deena Metzger describes as 'what it means to come into the animal presence'.

As such, it is a personal version of events. I have tried to report faithfully though, the experience, wisdom and knowledge of the team who worked with the leopards and the research of orthodox scientists.

Being personal, my message has a political imperative. The story is told from a position of hope that we move beyond our sense of human entitlement to a new way of relating to our planet and universe; of finding a way to respect all expressions of life. While we are different, we are equal. There are no lesser gods.

So, this book is also about reconciliation and the restoration of right relations between man and Nature.

I remain a messenger of this story, not its creator. I trust that its meaning will add to the critical mass building in the collective mind.

*Gillian van Houten*

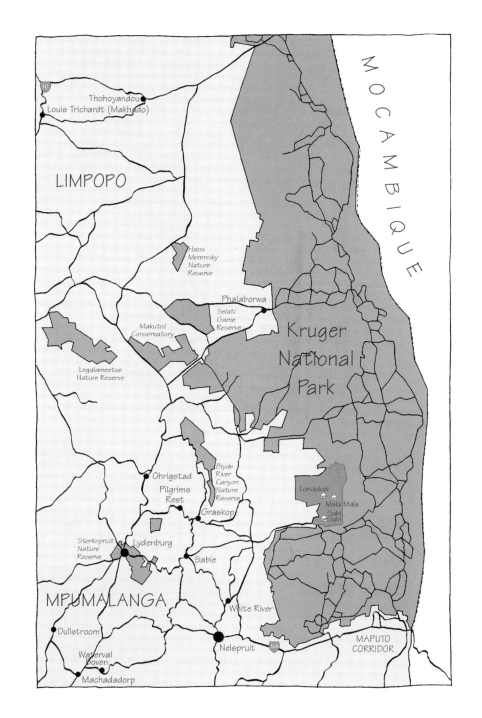

# CHAPTER ONE

# *The legacy of Mother Leopard*

She walked with more caution as she sensed the transition of night into day. The sky had lightened, almost imperceptibly. Sunrise was still some time off. It was not so much the changing of the light that alerted her to the shift in time, than that moment before dawn when all life is silent, when there is a pause between the haunting sounds of the African night and the rejoicing of the birds' dawn chorus ringing through the bush. The hyenas whooping in the distance fell silent. The owls hooting from the darkness of the trees were still. Among the lions, the soft grunting of the females as they sought one another; the roar of the males reverberating through the night proclaiming territory and dominance, ceased.

All of this informed her.

During the night, she had walked a distance of almost 15 kilometres from the place of her birth in the southeast of the conservancy. She had spent the first years of her life there. As she walked, she paused occasionally to gaze upwards at the stars, taking her direction from an inner guidance and those points of light. The constellation of Orion, the Great Hunter, rose in the east. The dull red glow of Betelgeuse pulsed like the beat of a heart alongside Sirius. The sickle moon hung low, new and without radiance.

Dark nights like this belong to predators, and she felt confident and strong in its shadows, her powers aligned to its coolness and energies. Curiously, for she was crossing into unknown territory, she moved with the sure tread of one who has an appointment to keep. There was youthfulness discernable in her movement, a slight lilt in her step, one could say some coquetry. A growing awareness of her sexuality. At three years old, she was undergoing a rite of passage, a young female leopard on the brink of maturity, seeking her own home range – to live, to hunt, to breed her cubs and to fulfil her destiny.

As dawn broke, her stride shortened. The previous fluid rolling motion of her shoulders gave way to a tenser, more angular movement, reflecting the vulnerability she felt. The early morning light exposed her position. She paused more often now, the slightest flick of the tip of her tail speaking mild apprehension, her body motionless as she assessed the changes around her and the dangers of daylight.

She rapidly ordered the details offered by the landscape. Hers was a world that went beyond the three-dimensional reality of the five senses. Hers was a world of nuance in sound and scent and light, of infinite variation in movement and rhythm; stories carried on the wind and whispered by the trees, a kaleidoscope of shifting energy fields and waves, the vibrational frequencies of all life forms around her.

Her padded paws moved silently across the sand of the dry river bed. With each step, lightly and then more firmly compressing the grains of sand, her distinctive tread conveyed to the earth a complex message, telling of her direction, her physical being and the subtleties of her state of mind. A supple flick of the wrist with each step, her deceptive feline softness concealing an immense power.

The first rays of daybreak slanted into the river bed through the acacia woodland, bearing traces of dust in the shafts of light. She chose the cover of the thorn thickets and outcrops of granite rocks, alternating her path between the shadows they cast across the sandy floor of the donga* and the secrecy of the rough and tangled grass that lined its edges. She remained unseen in the dappled play of sunlight, camouflaged by the earth-rich tones of her coat, patterned in perfect mimicry of Nature.

Despite her youth, she had already mastered the art of concealment. Leopards' ability to seemingly disappear is a power that goes beyond the physical adaptation of camouflage. There is more to it than this. It is some act of will, some mysterious conjuring ability with the physical realm. From being there, the leopard is suddenly not there.

As she emerged from the shadows and rounded a meander in the donga, where it intersected with a tributary, she heard the sound. Rather, the pre-cognition of sound, a subtle change in the vibration of the air currents. She crouched low, ears swivelling to trap the angle of its trajectory, to locate its direction and to fix its source.

She analysed the sound. It was human, mechanical in origin and advancing fast. She scanned the horizon methodically.

Suddenly from above, a grey loerie called 'kweh – h – h, go awaaaay', its cry of alarm revealing her presence. A group of vervet monkeys picking at jackalberries at the base of an ebony scampered up the trunk in fright, their black faces peeping out from behind the leaves to add their predator cry to the warning system of the bush.

There were two options open to her. She could scale the tall mahoganies with crowns of glossy, dark leaves that lined the river. Thickets of spike thorn, grewia and magic gwarrie bush lay ahead. Her decision made, she placed her back paw with deliberation in the tread of the leading one, as leopards do to avoid creating unnecessary sound, and crept over the lip of the donga into the clearing beyond. Then, she stepped into

* donga: trench erosion

the acacia woodland alongside the dirt road and waited.

John* had been out since before sunrise. He drove his battered Landrover down the dirt track alongside a dry riverbed – Princess Alice's donga – named after royalty who hunted lion in the early part of the century. This land had been in his family for three generations, a hunting farm in his father and grandfather's time. When John and his brother Dave became custodians after inheriting the land, they began nurturing the scrub-encroached land into a sanctuary for wildlife.

They called the game reserve 'Londolozi', which in Zulu means 'the protector of living things'. It lay at the heart of a vast, low-lying wilderness in the Mpumalanga region of South Africa, east of the mountain ranges of the interior escarpment. This lowveld* is an arid place of marginal rainfall; a dusty landscape patched into a mosaic of acacia thorn, mopani forest, scrub bush and scattered grasslands. Only the wilderness and its untamed creatures survive here, unyielding as the land is to all but nature's most resilient.

JV, as John is known, was deep in thought over the merits of their bush-clearing programme, a veld* management policy. This opened up the bush, allowing the grasses to re-seed themselves and flourish into pastures for grazing. Despite the earliness of the hour, the humidity was rising towards saturation. Absent-mindedly, he wiped his hand across his forehead and pulled the peak of his cap down deeper, to shield his eyes from the glare of the rising sun as he swung his vehicle eastwards. His binoculars hung loosely from the hook on the dashboard, his rifle lay in its mount at the front. He heard the cry of the grey loerie and the vervet monkeys. Knowing their predator call, he wondered if there might be hyena or lion passing by. Then, as he rounded a bend in the road, he slammed on brakes, drawing up sharply and sending a cloud of dust scattering from under the wheels.

There before him, in the shadows at the edge of the woodlands, a young leopard casually sharpened her claws on the bark of a scented thorn tree. He sat, barely daring to breathe, and watched, captivated. He had never before seen a wild leopard so confident in the presence of a human being. As a youngster, he had hunted leopards on this farm with his father. They were creatures of mystery, the stuff of fireside tales.

The leopard continued her private grooming ritual, absorbed in her task. He knew she was aware of his presence by her occasional sidelong glance at him and, as is the way of cats, seemingly ignoring him. She

*John Varty: wildlife film-maker *lowveld: low-lying bushveld *veld: bush

stretched her body sensuously, arching her spine low, as alternately she dug her claws into the soft bark of the tree and then retracted them, every now and then flexing her paws for a closer assessment of her work. She continued her manicure for a while, paying closer attention to this claw or that. Then, apparently content with her work, she skipped capriciously away into the bush. JV sat motionless in the Landrover, entranced by the young creature's tacit inclusion of him in her grooming ritual.

Sightings of leopard were rare when Londolozi began in 1974. The deep recesses of the bush and dense undergrowth of the habitat colluded with their secretive nature to conceal them. The best efforts of ingenious Shangaan trackers and highly skilled game rangers from the lodge could not locate them. While the leopards remained elusive, their presence could be felt in the tangible charge of the atmosphere when they were nearby.

Always, they remained out of sight. Tracks in the sand of the dry river beds told of their passing. The remains of carcasses found hoisted in the forked branches of trees revealed hunting success. Broken branches and scuff marks left in the sand of the thorn thickets spoke of drama. Occasionally, as a tourist vehicle made its way through the bush, there was a tantalizing glimpse of a rosetted coat receding into the scrub, prompting gasps of wonder and hope.

Mostly, the leopards remained apart, unrelenting in their seclusion. Only under cover of darkness would they emerge to enact their secret lives, to hunt or to mate, to defend their territories. And if the night was still, their rasping calls to one another could be heard over at the lodge in the hours between sunset and dawn, haunting, mysterious, and always beyond reach.

In the days that followed, drawn as if by a magnet, JV fervently searched the bush around Princess Alice's donga, yearning to once again be included in that circle of acceptance the young female leopard had extended to him. But leopards are not forthcoming by nature, and her demands were exacting. Determined to find her, JV approached Elmon Mhlongo, a Shangaan who lived in the village at Londolozi and worked as a tracker at the game reserve.

Elmon had grown up in a hunter-gatherer community in the area. His wizardry in reading the signs of the bush was legendary. His skills were those born of survival when, as a young boy in the bush, his life had depended on an accurate interpretation of spoor. A predator meant danger to his community and a threat to the few cattle and goats that they kept, while the passage of a herd of impala was an opportunity to hunt and eat. Through the teaching of his wily Uncle Engine, a notorious poacher, Elmon learned to identify animals from their tracks. In time, he saw beyond this simple descriptive information, seeing narrative and nuance in the stories relayed in the imprints of hoof and paw. After many years, he could shift his mind into being at one with the animal he was tracking, sensing many subtleties about it.

Together, JV and Elmon followed the young leopard's elusive trail; a broken twig here and there, the slightest depression in a patch of grass, strands of fur at the base of a tree, the occasional tread of her paw in the soft sand of the Mashabene* donga where she appeared to be setting up a territory.

Hers was to be a spoor that Elmon and JV came to know as intimately as their own signatures. All these clues spoke to them of her whereabouts and they began to catch fleeting glimpses of her. Their joy when they found her and she allowed them into her presence for a short while was inexpressible, a reward for days of single-minded searching through the inhospitable bush. And always, when she allowed them to approach, they kept a discreet distance should her fragile consent shatter through some disagreeable action of theirs.

Their tenacity and patience was tested as they followed the young female leopard. For days, weeks and months they waited for the trust that would allow them to stay close to her and gain more insight into the leopard's secretive world. After a while, they started to film her, following in the film vehicle night and day, watching her in wonder and learning from her. As a film-maker, JV recognised the uniqueness of such rare footage – a gift to receive with gratitude.

And so began a relationship between man and a wild leopard. A relationship that became obsession.

The young leopard was initially shy and occasionally hostile, but even in those early days JV sensed something unusual about her. She appeared to be assessing how safe she was with people. Often she seemed to expose her presence intentionally to the view of tourists and even showed them her cubs, gradually allowing more and more privilege. She drew towards her those who exchanged trust and those who came with goodwill in their hearts.

Their filming took on the rhythm of her life. Often there were nights where JV and Elmon would sleep in the film vehicle when the young leop-

*Mashabene: Shangaan word meaning 'place of sand'

ard lay down to rest, waking when she arose. Little by little she drew them into her world until they were a natural part of it, rejoicing with her through her triumphs of hunting, bearing cubs or outwitting her enemies, sharing her suffering with quiet respect.

Their reward was breathtaking footage of her flashing through the grasslands by moonlight, launching herself from ambush at startled prey, fluid as quicksilver. She was at one with the spirit of the trees, leaping with agility among their branches, a counterpoint of power and grace. Or hoisting prey of her own weight into a tree and wedging it to prevent piracy by hyenas. Her green eyes carried an unimaginable intelligence as they gazed at the world she encountered, seeing beyond the superficial. They would darken with passionate anger as she countered aggression towards herself or her cubs.

She was admired for her beauty, for her hunting strategies and survival tactics. But it was her unsurpassed skill as a mother that endeared her to those who came to know her. She produced nine litters of cubs and raised seventeen to independence, sharing with JV and Elmon on film and often with guests, intimate moments – her mating, her maternal tenderness and her transparent delight at the antics of her cubs. She became known as 'Mother Leopard', and began to assume the status of legend. Foreign tourists carried stories about her to the far corners of the world. In their encounters with Mother Leopard, tourists felt that something unique and intimate had passed between them.

Over the years with JV and Elmon, Mother Leopard's attitude of tolerance developed into one of acceptance. Their unusual working partnership thrived and grew towards an empathetic trust, a tentative contact across the barrier of species.

One night, JV and Elmon were filming Mother Leopard as she hunted along the Mashabene donga, close to the heart of her territory. The terrain was overgrown with tight clumps of tatawa, haak-en-steek* and thickets of scented thorn – formidable terrain for manoeuvring an open-backed film vehicle. For Mother Leopard it was ideal habitat. She could conceal herself as she slowly edged her way towards prey on the opposite clearing.

Her hunt that night was assisted by a strong wind that gusted sporadically, throwing up the dust and distorting the sounds of the bushveld into unfamiliar patterns. The impala were noticeably nervous, huddling together and twitching their ears uneasily this way and that, unsure of the haphazard

*haak-en-steek: Afrikaans word for the umbrella thorn acacia

and scrambled messages carried on the wind. Mother Leopard advanced with the disturbance of sound, then paused motionless in the lull. Darkness was on her side. The moon was a thin sliver and the patches of clouds scudding across the stars concealed all ambient light. She blended like a shadow into the blackness of the night.

Her eyes were fixed on a young impala at the edge of the group, more uneasy than the rest of the herd, and in its distraction, moving slightly apart. She held her focus firmly on the white blaze of its tail, her instincts and perceptions melding into a finely tuned unity. Keeping low to the ground, she swiftly crossed into the clearing. As a hunter, the leopard is the quintessential stalker-pouncer. She needed to get close, within five or ten metres, before she pounced.

Unlike the lion that can run down its prey in a chase, she would more often than not abort her attack if her prey became alerted to her presence and bolted before she could leap at its throat.

For film-makers, such a situation is a delicate one. They must be careful not to give advantage to predator or prey by the positioning of the film vehicle, or heightened visibility to either in the sweep of the spotlights. Personal instinct and experience needs to harmonise with that of the predator to read her tactics and timing, swinging into action with lights and cameras fractionally after the predator makes the fatal pounce. Timing is everything. Move a second too soon and the prey is alerted, a second too late and the scene is lost.

JV crouched low over his camera, the back of his shirt wet with perspiration in the humidity of the night, muscles tense, his concentration unwavering despite his fatigue. Elmon sat at the wheel, his senses alive to the moment, eyes straining in the dark, moving in his mind along the grassland with Mother Leopard as she crawled closer and closer towards the impala. He waited for the moment, as he had done so many times before, when he would sense her muscles bunch as she drew in her energies, sinking low into a crouch before the lethal pounce.

Suddenly, the two men swung around as one, their attention caught by a slight rustling. Something had disturbed a bush on the far side of their vehicle. Their hearts sank as they drew breath in alarm.

'Ngala!'* Elmon whispered.

Not a hundred metres away, a lioness moving opportunistically through the grassland entered the clearing, her presence undetected by Mother Leopard. The two were mortal enemies and an attack was

*Ngala: Shangaan word meaning 'lion'

inevitable. The lioness's gaze locked on her rival, her tail flicked once or twice in irritation and then, seizing the moment, her powerful body tensed. She dropped low and moving into a menacing stalk, slipped out of sight behind a termite mound in ambush.

JV cursed under his breath. Surely Mother Leopard would sense her rival? But so intent was her concentration on the final moments of her own hunt that all her attention was focused there. As she moved closer to the termite mound, the lioness leapt out at her, going directly for her throat in a flash of tawny fur and fury, pinning the leopard to the ground, her raucous growl of victory reverberating through the night.

'Hamba!' JV shouted terse, desperate instructions to Elmon, 'Hamba kakhulu!'*

Elmon's foot hit the accelerator. The Landrover lurched forward crazily through the grass, engine screaming and lights flashing. He drove directly at the two cats writhing on the ground. Mother Leopard was fighting desperately for her life against the lioness, so much more powerful than she. The pitch of the revving engine alarmed the lioness. She jerked her head back involuntarily from the leopard, releasing her grip to snarl at the vehicle coming headlong at her. In that split second, Mother Leopard wrested herself free from certain death and leapt up a nearby marula tree, leaving the defeated lioness to lope off into the night.

Stunned, the two men sat silently in their vehicle beneath the tree. JV reflected on his impulsive intervention. Until then, he had never transgressed the wildlife film-maker's code of detachment, to observe but not interfere with the processes of nature. He knew that Mother Leopard had tiny cubs waiting for her in her den. More than likely they would be hungry and expecting their mother's return from her hunt, unaware of her near demise not a hundred yards from them.

JV and Elmon had detected Mother Leopard's lair a few days previously in the Mashabene donga, after observing a pattern in her movements. For three months since she had mated with the territorial male, they had awaited the birth of her cubs, watching her belly as it grew to roundness. Then, the licked and matted fur around her swollen teats told them that the cubs had arrived. Eager to see the newborns and hoping to film them in the den, JV and Elmon trudged up and down the length of the dry river bed, searching all the likely den sites; a useful brush pile, a thicket of thorn, a deep crevice in an outcrop of boulders. Finally, hidden in the depths of a washed-away root system of a gnarled and ancient tree, they found the newborn cubs.

*Hamba kakhulu!: Zulu expression meaning 'Go quickly'

JV knelt in the sand of the donga before the tiny, mewing creatures. Elmon stood guard in case Mother Leopard should return from hunting and misinterpret their actions. One of the cubs edged forward on its puny legs, wobbling precariously. It nuzzled in close to JV's body sensing his warmth and attempted to suckle on his sweatshirt. He sat enraptured, camera discarded beside him, honoured beyond measure that the tiny creature had mistaken him momentarily for its mother.

And then, as the cub's better judgement registered, it erupted into a fireball of hissing, spitting fury and retreated with its sibling into the recesses of the den. They flattened themselves into its crevices and froze, invisible from view. After a moment, JV and Elmon walked back along the donga to the film vehicle, beaming from ear to ear with the silliest of expressions on their faces.

Was that it? Was it the contact with the cubs that had driven JV to intervene in the fight he had just witnessed? He sat in his film vehicle and smiled wryly to himself in the darkness, wondering what had happened to his impartiality as he recognised some barrier falling within himself. Quite simply, in helping Mother Leopard, he had saved the life of a friend and in doing so, he had given her cubs a second chance.

It was past midnight when the men drove back to base camp and JV dropped Elmon off at his home in the village. Afterwards, JV sat alone in the early hours of the morning unravelling events, trying to make some sense of his intervention. The earlier gusting of the wind had settled. All was still. The clouds had cleared from the sky and the stars shone with brilliance and clarity. As if in synchronicity with the clearing and settling of the atmosphere, the discord in his mind subsided and his thoughts formed with lucidity. JV knew in that moment that had Mother Leopard died in her encounter with the lioness, he would have done what was unthinkable in terms of accepted wildlife management practice. He would have searched out and rescued the cubs and raised them for her.

Right then and there, an idea was born.

He decided that one day, when Mother Leopard's life was over, he would adopt two leopard cubs from a wildlife refuge and raise them. It would be a way of continuing the process of human and leopard interaction that had begun with her. Filming the story of the cubs' lives would give him a vehicle through which to tell the story of the remarkable Mother Leopard. She had allowed him a glimpse at the secret life of her kind, teaching him about leopards and creating in him a fascination for wild cats that would stay with him for a lifetime. To tell her story and what she had shared with him would be JV's tribute to their time together and his way of honouring her life.

\* \* \*

I do not remember quite when it was that I was drawn into the mystique that surrounded Mother Leopard. My early days with the big cats in the wilderness were largely blurred by awe. Before coming to work at Londolozi with JV and Elmon, to write about wildlife and to shoot photographs, I had lived in Johannesburg. My career in communications revolved around photojournalism and the hectic world of current affairs television. I was so captivated by the drama and adventure of life in the bush that for a long while I was distracted from the more subtle and far-reaching dynamics of what existed between Mother Leopard and my new colleagues.

The door of awareness she opened was not attached to any particular event, but was more the evolution of piecing together unexplained ideas and random insights that came to me in the presence of the big cats.

I have vivid memories of my first summer in the bush – the searing heat of the days that stretched unrelentingly into the night. Hot and damp with humidity and perspiration, we followed Mother Leopard in the film vehicle as she hunted through the bush, determined not to lose her. Elmon drove the vehicle and shone the spotlights while JV and I sat in the back with our mounted cameras, ducking to avoid overhanging thorn branches as we wound our way through dense woodlands of acacia thorn.

Often our pursuit would become frantic when we had to drive the long way round a drainage line which she had cut through, or when she increased her pace. Saplings snapped back in the wake of our vehicle, cracking like rifle shots in the darkness of the night. Francolins exploded in shrieking outrage from our path as the wheels of the vehicle churned through the grass releasing the moist, dank scents of the undergrowth.

When the terrain became impassable and JV urged Elmon to drive on, I gripped the handrail, white-knuckled, as we catapulted across grasslands fraught with ditches. Often I would find myself staring wide-eyed as the vehicle skidded wildly across the floor of a dry river bed, or lurched on an unlikely slope, engine whining, the back or the front wheels spinning freely above the ground. Then, after taking a few moments to collect ourselves and our scattered equipment, we'd be off again after Mother Leopard. She, in contrast to our comic inelegance, slipped gracefully and with silent ease through the bush.

In the less frantic moments, waiting in the long hours of those nights, every conceivable variety of insect and moth swirled or fluttered in the spotlight we used for filming. Mosquitoes droned in swarms, the atmosphere alive with the sounds of the African night. Around us, innumerable cicadas called in their shrill, vibrating tones.

In the distance, hippos grunted their irritations and contentments, while closer to us, from the clearing, the piercing whistle of a water dikkop cut through the air. A rustle and a scurry in the undergrowth told of an unseen creature of the night. Then, as a message passed through the inhabitants of the bush, a silence would descend around us as Mother Leopard's presence became known. On nights like these I had never seen the sky more liquid black or believed there were so many stars in the heavens. In the bushveld, everything pulsated with a tangible rhythm, which resonated through me. I felt a vitality and exhilaration I had seldom known.

My esteem for JV and Elmon was limitless. Neither heat, mosquitoes, the hours of waiting, the fatigue, nor the frustration seem to faze them. Sometimes the air turned blue with cursing at our own human error in missing a sequence on film. Nothing that Mother Leopard asked was too much.

At first, I found the physical strains of working in the bush exhausting. I found the frustration of the work harder to cope with and often I would wipe away hot, secret tears. We seemed to have so little control over filming Mother Leopard. Nevertheless, it led me to appreciate JV and Elmon's tenacity and commitment to communicating their insights on film.

In many ways, there were similarities between the men and the leopards: in Elmon, an intuition bordering on the mystical and in JV, an exterior detachment, concealing a passionate nature and a determination of steel.

In the bushveld at midday, the humidity bore down like a physical weight, creating an eerie silence as its inhabitants paused to conserve energy. Later, towards the afternoon, we walked, tracking through thicket, grassland and dry river bed to locate Mother Leopard in preparation for the night's film work.

More often than not, JV and Elmon communicated in silence, through the slightest gesture of hand or head. When they followed separate spoor, a low whistle in varying tones or the click of a finger indicated their position. I had learned something about following spoor, but often could see nothing before me. What were they seeing where no indication of a track lay? How did they know to turn this way or that? And then, sometimes with neither word nor gesture passing between them, they would simultaneously give up on the track, jump into the Landrover and drive elsewhere. The basic skeleton of their ideas was communicated in silence – any descriptive fleshing out in words passed telepathically. Through some mysterious process they had absorbed some of the ways of the leopard.

I seldom spoke at times like these, reluctant to show my ignorance and trusting that in time I too would come to understand this mute language. I learnt early on the extent to which the human voice carries in the bush and the dissonance it creates. I learned how speech corrupts the other senses and compromises the flow of the more subtle suggestions from our instinct and intuition.

Elmon and JV didn't always know the answers. Mother Leopard still had her secrets. When something about her behavior puzzled us, I offered initially what I thought might be a helpful comment, quoting from some field study. JV and Elmon listened and nodded encouragingly. Often we smiled in disbelief at the gulf between the textbook and the insights of particularity from direct experience, and the teaching coming from Mother Leopard. Although I was a novice in wildlife, the discipline of thorough research I brought from my career was my contribution. This and my habit of questioning a situation from all angles was to assist in time with glimpses of understanding.

Curiously, while our lessons were ostensibly about leopards, they were simultaneously about humility and limitation, about respecting sanctity. When Mother Leopard chose to be alone, we never found her. After hours, even days of absence, once again there she would be.

In those early days, I felt that sometimes I was just not getting it when we were in Mother Leopard's presence. At first I put it down to being a newcomer on the team, distanced by the bonds of partnership between JV and Elmon. In tight moments, each in turn had saved the other's life. Gradually, I came to realise that the feeling had more to do with Mother Leopard. I was party to something much larger than merely making a film about a leopard. I was witnessing the subtle dynamics between two men and a leopard. Theirs was a shared history of reciprocity and trust. The men had come to understand the complexities of the individual she was, the nuances of her mind, the shades of her personality. They had shared in her successes and failures, her joys and sorrows. Access to this privilege was not automatic. I understood with humility that first I would need to pay my dues and demonstrate my own goodwill.

Living closely with leopards, so much of what happens hovers in a world of hints and guesses. I became aware of a thought moving at the edge of my consciousness. It was rooted in a subtle change in tone when we moved into Mother Leopard's presence.

After the excitement of the pursuit, a calm would settle over JV. Beyond the simple success of having located her and confirmed her well-being, something more was being affirmed. Something larger.

JV is a man oriented to action and, while the commitments in him run deep, he is not given to theoretical speculation. I was curious when he described being in the presence of Mother Leopard as a 'spiritual experience'. I began to wonder if, through our connection with this wild creature, some invisible pathway was being facilitated. Was Mother Leopard throwing a lifeline to us, our self-excluded and lonely human selves who, in our ignorance, had set ourselves apart from Nature? In our attempts to control, had we alienated ourselves from the source of our being? Could Mother Leopard be reconnecting us to that state of grace in Nature where all life exists in harmony, where creatures live in right relation with one another? There were moments when these unorthodox thoughts no longer felt sharply strange, but like something long-forgotten, stirred to memory, fleeting, not quite within my grasp.

I sensed something else. As I became immersed in the natural world, drawn there largely by Mother Leopard, life seemed to flow and meld more easily than in my urban existence. A more complex tune played through my days than one of simple cause and effect. Everywhere there were patterns of intertwined purpose and meaning. There was the constant sense of an underlying presence, moving through everything.

What I expected when I first came to Londolozi was the savagery, the magnificence, and the extremes. Nature red in tooth and claw. I observed with astonishment, and some amusement, the neat preconceptions that I had made. I had perceived the wilderness as a thing apart, with its own distinct laws. At the end of a session with Mother Leopard, we would pack up and go 'home'. While I moved between these seemingly separate worlds of the wilderness and human culture, I began to sense them merging. I began to discover the complexity within Mother Leopard and to identify with her in a way I hadn't imagined possible.

Initially, I recoiled from the hard-edged reality. What did it mean to live the way she did? Life and death so intricately balanced and so basic in its drives: the aggression of inter-predator rivalry; the seclusion in solitary ways; the flailing, kicking finality of the kill; the bloody physicality of death in torn throats, flesh ripped open and devoured warm and throbbing, the fetid smell of intestines.

But Mother Leopard also showed me the infinitely gentle side of Nature. I came to understand the grace and purity of the hunt, the piety of her obedience. I couldn't imagine anything softer than the velvet fur of that same muzzle that killed with such efficiency. Or ever seeing a gaze more poignant than when her eyes, at first downcast, swept upwards to the stars in a dreamlike state, the privacy of her thoughts denied us. And when she greeted her son with a rub of the head, cheek to cheek, and they lay together in companionship soaking up the slow warmth of a winter's morning, often a look of aching tenderness would pass between them. It brought tears to my eyes.

I came to know Mother Leopard towards the end of her life. She had a single male cub at the time, almost two years old, handsome and fast approaching maturity with powerful muscles thickening in his neck and shoulders. Proudly she would sit with him, eyes half-closed in pleasure, tolerant beyond measure of his clownish tactics when he stalked her tail as she flicked the tip. After reading the data we kept, I understood that she was holding on to him beyond the time when she had vigorously dispersed her earlier litters. She appeared to be anchoring her last son by feeding him excessively. With his belly extended and a sleepy look of complete satiation, she would lead him to another kill she had stored in a tree elsewhere. Perhaps she needed the companionship, or was it the protection his presence gave her?

I began to suspect that Mother Leopard sensed her end was near and was acting it out in her relationship with her cub, by holding him to her. Aware that she couldn't produce any more offspring, she was reluctant to let go of her last.

Mother Leopard lived to 17, an advanced age for a leopard in the wild. Her reflexes became fractionally slower and slower, her senses minutely losing their edge. It was those few seconds that cost her her life. In her eighteenth year and twice within the space of a few months, lions attacked her. Miraculously, she survived the first attack. Her wounds healed but left her with a stiffness in her back legs, which slowed her reactions even further. The second attack came almost as soon as she had recovered from the first. This time the mauling was severe.

We tracked her to a termite mound behind a thorn thicket. She had concealed herself to rest and nurse her wounds – a gaping gash to her right flank. She looked so old and frail, this magnificent creature that had lived with such power and vitality. The immense skill she showed in hunting, raising her cubs and pure survival had raised her life to myth. I had come to believe that she was as indestructible as the legend she had become.

I was filled with sadness for us all, especially for JV who had known her so closely and for so long and whose anguish at her condition was tangible. In the days following this attack, he was restless and distracted, faced as he was with the inevitable. Mother Leopard was dying. He sat with her for long hours in his film vehicle, defending her from the hyenas which, given the chance, would close in on her in her weakened state. His presence allowed her the dignity in death that was rightfully hers. Silently he sat alongside her, urging her towards life.

He took meat and water to sustain her. There is no creature in the African bush more ferocious or dangerous than a wounded leopard, yet painfully she dragged herself forward and accepted his offering, drinking deeply from the water and trying courageously to eat the meat. She allowed JV to approach her more closely than ever before, but he kept a respectful distance. And as the days passed, Mother Leopard rested in the protection he offered her.

On the last day of this silent vigil, rain began to fall. JV thought he noticed Mother Leopard rally. She appeared to become calmer and more composed, so he returned to base camp to store his camera equipment out of the rain.

During his absence, JV lost her.

Mother Leopard slipped away as quietly and mysteriously as she had come. He never saw her again. She left no tracks. The rain washed them away. Her body was never found, despite an extensive search by master trackers. For JV, the pain of losing her was that of losing a beloved friend. Over 12 years they had travelled a long path together.

And now, Mother Leopard was dead.

# CHAPTER TWO

# *Yebo, zingwe ezincane*

*Greetings, little leopards!*

We'd arranged to collect them from the customs office at Bulawayo Airport in Zimbabwe. Their travelling box was surprisingly small. It was painted a gaudy shade of green and looked insignificant among the other parcels and packages waiting on the counter. Only the airholes on the side of the box told of the presence of some living creature within. Inside that box were two six-week-old leopard cubs, male and female, that were to come home to live at Londolozi.

A makeshift hessian curtain hung down loosely over the mesh grid on one side of the box, concealing its contents and protecting sensitive eyes from the harsh light. I resisted drawing back the cloth to look inside at the two little newcomers. We had waited years for this moment and now they were before me. I wanted to meet them straight away. But not in the customs office. Too many people clamoured to complete their business, too much distraction and noise. Instead, I clung protectively to the box as we made our way through the red tape of the immigration and customs bureaucracy, sorting out the paperwork and the permits that govern the lives of animals in transit.

Soon we were back inside our aeroplane, taxiing down the runway for the flight home. The safety belt held the green box with its cargo perched beside us. I waited for the high-pitched revving of the engines to settle into a quieter hum as the aeroplane reached cruising altitude. Then at last I drew back the hessian curtain.

Huddled against the side of the box was a confusion of straw and spotted fur. In an instant two tousled heads popped up and two pairs of large and liquid blue-grey eyes stared intently. For a moment they held my gaze, their expression almost blank, verging on astonishment. Then, at once a fury of hissing and spitting erupted, as two cubs scrambled in retreat to the farthest corner of the box and glared at me with hostility.

The smaller of the two was the female, her body slighter and more graceful, her features more delicate, distinguishing her from her brother, even at this young age. She was also the more defensive of the two, stamping against the floor of the box in a rage and snarling with a ferocity that contradicted her tiny size. The young male cub, initially startled, appeared to be overcome by curiosity. His hissing became half-hearted and then stopped altogether, as his fear gave way to fascination. He gazed at us, tilting his head this way and that, trying to make some sense of his new circumstances. After a short while he fell asleep, mid-stride between conflicting ideas about whether we were friend or foe.

It was a four-hour flight from Bulawayo back to Londolozi, including the South African border stop at Musina to clear customs. We had started out before dawn that morning and, as the day wore on, midday heat and the drone of the aeroplane engines soon lulled our group into quiet thoughtfulness or light sleep. I sat gazing from the window at the countryside below.

Beneath us lay a landscape ravaged by the drought of successive seasons. A bitter drought, deep into the cycle of scarcity and plenty – the destiny of Africa. Rain had fallen the previous summer and when the clouds burst, deliverance came at the point of desperation. As I looked over the land, I could see here and there the miracle of nature unfolding as the land responded to the life-giving rain. Flushes of green emerged between the patches of dry, red dust and the fields of blackened and shrivelled crops.

After the death of Mother Leopard three years earlier, we tried to deal with the sadness of our loss by focusing our energies on the film JV wanted to make to honour her life. How best to do this? We took our lead from the inspiration JV had the night of her near fatal clash with the lioness, when he and Elmon saved her life. We would tell her story in retrospect from that critical moment when she might have died and left two newborn cubs orphaned in her den. So, we needed to find two leopard cubs.

So often in our work we hear of orphaned or abandoned creatures found in the wild, with no hope of a life of freedom. Often, their future lies in captivity. Now we could offer the opportunity of freedom to two young leopard cubs in such a situation. We planned to film Mother Leopard's life through the eyes of these cubs as we released them into the wild and monitored their progress. In this way we would carry on the work of learning about leopards.

There are frequent reports of farmers shooting stock-marauding leopards. Snares too, laid by poachers, take their toll, as do hunters seeking rosetted skin trophies. The cubs are often victims. For some inexplicable reason, the aggressors, having murdered the leopard mothers, balk at killing the cubs. They go out of their way to present the orphans at zoos or rehabilitation centres, usually with shifty-eyed explanations as to how they came by them. One of the most far-fetched stories we heard during our search for cubs was that of a mother leopard being 'knocked down by a train' as she sat on a railway line. The 'onlookers' had no choice but to present the cubs, which they had discovered crying pitifully in their den, to the local zoo.

But, for two long years there was no response to our offer, despite an exhaustive search among our wildlife contacts. Our correspondence files grew until they bulged, but no cubs. And then, finally, an offer of two cubs came. Not orphans, but bred in captivity at a wildlife exhibition centre in Zimbabwe. News of our intended release project had fallen on fertile ground.

The pitch of the engines fell and the aircraft began to descend for landing at Musina, a remote airstrip just inside the northern border of South Africa. After the aircraft shuddered to a halt, we opened the doors, expecting to be greeted by customs officials. The place was deserted and a silence closed in around us. We wandered around, investigated a few drably painted buildings, but they were all locked and shuttered. There was nothing else to do but to sit in the patchy shade of a solitary marula tree at the edge of the runway and wait for the officials to arrive to stamp our papers. The windsock on the airstrip hung limp in the still, oppressive heat. All that moved was a hazy mirage rising off the tar.

After waiting for a while, I crossed to the aeroplane to make sure the cubs' box was in the shade. I heard a single, plaintive mewing sound. How could I reassure the cubs? Should I do anything at all? Would intervening make matters worse? With their stress, I knew they wouldn't take any food or water. The most logical response seemed to be to leave them alone until we were home at Londolozi, where we could release them to run freely in the safety of their boma*.

But a deeper instinct in me responded to the forlorn mewing. How terrified the cubs must be, no matter how wild or hostile. I crouched down next to the box. After a pause, I spoke in soft, low tones hoping to convey a sense of calm. But no. Another thin wail rose from within.

Resolutely, I opened the box and reached in, fully expecting my hand to be bitten or scratched to shreds by needle-like claws and teeth. I lifted the first cub firmly by the scruff of its neck – it was the male. My hand took hold around the loose skin at the back of his neck, as a mother leopard does when carrying her cubs. His wiry, squirming body went limp as he acquiesced. I drew the creature close to me and held him in the curve of my neck and shoulder where he could feel the beat of my pulse.

His fur was soft and woolly against my skin. I smelt the sharp scent of his wildness and felt his heart pounding against his rib cage. He nestled

*boma: protected enclosure in the bush

in close and there I held him. It was only for a brief moment, yet with the intensity of life finding life, despite the barrier of species, it seemed to span eternity.

I looked up smiling towards the rest of our group, and read the near-panic on JV's face. I could see what he was thinking. All we needed now was to have our precious leopard cubs escaping and darting wildly around this forlorn airstrip in the middle of nowhere. For the moment, practicality would need to prevail over what a deeper knowledge had guided me to do. I put the young male back in the box. By the sounds of the spitting and snarling inside, which accompanied his return, his sister's outrage was reaching epic proportions.

But something happened in that brief moment of holding. Through the mute but articulate language of touch, I felt I had reached the self within the wild and frightened cub. I knew by his submission to what comfort I could offer him with my body, and its warmth of living energy, that he too had experienced a similar connection beyond my human form.

I imagined how it might be for the cubs. The day had begun like most other days in their short lives, filled with wide-eyed innocence and springy games at their mother's side in their cage. Suddenly, their mother was gone. They were just six weeks old and they were alone. They were trapped in a small, square space, one they had entered eagerly, scenting the promise of food. Once inside and having eaten the food, escape was denied. Together, they huddled in their misery of fear and confusion. The scattering of straw on the floor offered them little opportunity to bury themselves. Every so often, the box would lurch unexpectedly, sending them sprawling in an inelegant slide as they made futile efforts to gain a grip on its unyielding surface.

Human sounds sent them scurrying to the far reaches of the box. At the wildlife centre they had been familiar with human scent, but experienced it at their mother's side as she moved her body in front of them to shield them. Now they were alone and exposed, so they huddled quietly together, drawing what little comfort they could from each other's touch and presence.

After a time, they began to move around the box, sniffing it here and there in the hopes of discovering some clue as to what they should do, straining their eyes in the darkness towards the shafts of light which slant-ed in through the airholes. Their ears swivelled constantly, desperate to catch some familiar sound beyond the stillness.

The explosive sound of an engine blasted into life, its all-consuming noise and vibration deafening them, the overpowering fumes it belched forth robbing them of their senses. They tensed their bodies into a crouch and spat viciously in all directions, not knowing where the attack was coming from. They were without comprehension, save their mutual certainty of danger.

The young female was distraught and anxious for her brother, who didn't seem to be taking the nature of their plight seriously enough. Finally, an unbearably bright light flashed across her eyes, almost blinding her. Through it she managed to make out a human face peering directly at her.

She had never been that close to a human before. She knew from within herself what she must do. Every hair of her body stood on end, enlarging the size of her overall appearance. Her eyes glowed demonically as her pupils dilated with a mixture of defensive animosity and fear. Adrenalin surged through her body, preparing for the fight with the human she would have to face. Cornered, she prepared to harness the energy of her fear. Like a supreme martial artist, she would transmute it into a single-minded counter-attack, in the manner that has given the leopard the reputation of being the most feared cat in the wild.

Her brother, although alarmed, was not reacting with the same level of fear. His oscillated with an overwhelming curiosity. What was going on? He was puzzled by conflicting messages around him. His sister's panic and the urgency of her message had drawn him into defence mode. But when the threat did not materialise into any tangible form, he felt the need to investigate. He edged forward, tentatively sniffing the box and trying to peer through the holes on its side.

As he stood there, gingerly sniffing at the grid of the box, an ear-shattering growl, deep-throated and malevolent, came from behind him, accompanied by a furious stamping sound. In his heightened state of alertness, the shock was too much for him. He leapt four-legged off the ground, bumping his head hard on the roof of the box, then fell dazed to the ground. He scrambled to his feet and turned around, ready to confront the danger approaching from behind.

He saw his sister before him, her ears pulled flat, lips drawn back, contorting her face into a vicious snarl, her body coiled taut in preparation for attack. That awful growl was coming from her throat! He stared at her, lost in admiration at her ferocity. Perhaps he should growl too? But the little rumble that came from his throat could hardly be heard above his sister's terrible noises. He tried to improve. Just then the box lurched sideways again and sent him sprawling to its side, squashing his face up against the airholes.

Through these holes he saw all sorts of curious things. Strangely too, the harsh chattering of human beings that had made him so nervous earlier was no longer causing him such distress. Something had changed in the tone. He strained his ears to listen beyond his sister's ongoing, menacing growl.

Through the airholes from beyond the box came a soft, low voice. As he listened, he grew more and more fascinated. It was a human voice, but its tones were gentle. He imagined the voice was directed at him. Then once again, his sister's passionate anger refocused his fear. Once more he was distracted by the voice he felt sure was calling him. The confusion was too much to cope with. He felt himself becoming very, very tired. He yearned for his mother, for the strength of her body and the certainty of her guidance. A forlorn cry rose to his throat and then, as if in answer to his call, he felt himself swept up gently by the scruff of his neck in the way that his mother held him in her mouth.

He was saved! He acquiesced, letting go of his fear, as he found himself gathered into the protective warmth of a pulsating, living embrace. Despite the overwhelming scent of human, he lay quite still and heard the familiar gurgling noises he had heard from within his mother's body. And there, yes, there also, was the reassuring rhythm of a heartbeat, strong and sure.

As sunset reddened the sky over the Drakensberg escarpment, an aeroplane approached from the fiery western rim, heading towards the vast, flat lands of the lowveld. On board, asleep, two young leopard cubs lay entwined. How were they to know that fate had selected them to participate in a story that had begun many years before with the mother leopard of Londolozi? Their journey would take them from the captivity of their birth to a future that was wild and free. Along the way they would tell the story of Mother Leopard, and continue along the pathway she had forged during her lifetime.

The plane flew into the gathering dusk of Londolozi. We were expected at T'Ingwe tented camp, built at the confluence of the Mashabene and Inyatini* dongas, the cubs' new home.

The campsite had been carefully selected. The area around it was filled

*Inyatini: Shangaan word meaning 'the place of the buffalo'

23

with secretive half-light and shadow. Soft sand in the dry river bed made for silent passage. It was an ideal habitat for leopards. Dense riverine vegetation lined the banks of the donga. Tall Transvaal mahoganies and sturdy-boughed jackalberries reached above acacia thorn thickets, clumps of shrub and tangled titawa creeper. Nyala, bushbuck and kudu browsed in these thickets and beyond, as the vegetation thinned to open grassland, were herds of impala, zebra and waterbuck. This had been the home of Mother Leopard, where she had given birth to her cubs in the seclusion of tree trunks, rock piles or recesses in root systems lining the dry river bed. Here she had hunted from the ambush of termite mounds and tree stumps in the woodlands.

Our project team would live here in T'Ingwe* camp for a year with the cubs. It was the closest way we could live in their world while they participated in ours.

Many arduous hours had gone into preparing the camp. Patches of shrub and low-lying bush were cleared for the tents, bucket showers erected and drop toilets dug. As we worked, the Shangaan crew from the village broke out into spontaneous bursts of work songs. Deep, resonant voices chanted in unison, drawing rhythm from the hammering of the tent pegs or the strike of the pickaxe. A chant led by a solo voice for the upswing of the pick invited a collective response, as the axe swung through its arc to strike the earth. Instructions and requests were shouted above the clamour, often several voices at once. The passionate nature of the Shangaan language finds expression in the simplest of statements. To an outsider, a straightforward question 'Hey, where's my bottle of water?' can sound like a heated argument. Eventually, chaos gave way to order and T'Ingwe camp was ready. More or less …

The camp was on a slight rise, with a good view down both branches of the donga. The sleeping tents were pitched in a close arc around the cubs' boma for their protection in the hope that our human presence would fend off any curious passing animals. The mess tent, as well as the entrance to the camp, was at the opposite side, to keep all disruptions and noise away from the cubs. Their boma was a large wire mesh and thorn branch enclosure, lined with soft river sand, designed to keep danger out and the cubs from wandering off without protection.

JV, Elmon and I needed a reliable and committed back-up team. Two newcomers, Karin and Graham, were hired for the film crew. Their job would be to attend to the daily business of the camp and to the immedi-

*T'Ingwe: Shangaan word meaning 'leopard'

ate needs of the cubs. To help them, Lawrence and Andries came from the Shangaan village near the lodge.

As with Elmon, these two brothers operated from a rural tribal mind-set, completely different from the western way where animals are viewed as a thing apart. Their perspective was of a shared world where life flowed with connectivity. The forces that governed life and death were bound up with dreams, magic and the guiding hand of ancestors.

Graham was a former game ranger from Londolozi, with a natural love of the wilderness and its creatures. He had good bush knowledge and while guiding tourists had learnt much about leopards. He was competent with a camera, rifle and radio and was trained to deal with the unexpected hazards of the bush.

Karin was an aspirant wildlife film-maker, newly graduated from film school and fresh from travel adventures around the world. She was a strong, gentle person with a calm temperament, ideally suited to working with animals. When I collected her from the lodge, she swung her multi-coloured backpack into the Landrover and we drove out to T'Ingwe camp. It was difficult to keep a conversation going as she broke it off continually with 'oohs' and 'aahs' of wonder at the sight of the bushveld. Her eyes widened as we worked our way around a pride of lions sleeping in the road and drove through fields of burnished oat grass with giraffe grazing off the buffalo thorn. They were so close to our vehicle you could almost touch them.

Our talk around the campfire the night we arrived with the cubs was softened by overtones of awe. A tangible current of excitement ran through the conversation, quickening the pulse of all gathered there. As it rose and fell, eyes shone in the reflected flicker of firelight in anticipation of the journey ahead. An early autumn wind sang softly around the ropes and canvas flaps and gusted occasionally down the Inyatini donga, rustling the dry and fallen leaves.

From the dark recesses of the giant ebony tree, which held its branches protectively over the camp, came the persistent hoot of a pearl-spotted owl. In Shangaan lore, its presence was a benevolent ancestor made manifest and watching the unfolding events with curiosity. In the sky, the moon rising towards fullness was in Libra, an aspect that releases in abundance the nurturing energies of partnership and reciprocity. From the darkness of the night, its light fell on the campfire scene below in a luminous glow.

There, in the wilderness of the African bush, in a tented camp pitched at the edge of the dry river bed that was once the heart of Mother Leopard's home range, a joining was in process, a tentative reaching out of one species towards another in mutual discovery.

*Right:* Little Boy and Little Girl curl up
with Lion and Leppie.
*Below:* Little Girl was overcome with
exhaustion after her long journey.

*Left: At three months old, the cubs look apprehensively at the big, wide world.*

*Above:* Ears flattened, Little Girl shows the fear and hostility she felt when she came to live with us.
*Left:* Little Girl indulges in a rare moment of affection from her beloved brother.

*Above:* Playing with leopards can earn you a scratch or two!
*Top right:* The cubs practise the art of concealment in a rocky outcrop.
*Right:* Keeping records of weight gain was a tricky business.
*Far right:* Little Boy takes a closer look at our bush toilet.

Left: The cubs fight for possession of JV's sandals.
Above left: Me and JV with the cubs. At first everything felt strange, even holding the cubs.
Above right: Little Girl, very proud of the boot she has 'killed'.
Below left: Leopards are not generally cuddly, only sometimes.
Below right: The cubs remained curious about our camera gear. Little Girl sniffs at my lens brush.

**Above and top right:** *Little Girl hunting catfish.*
**Middle right:** *Elmon and JV take their first shots of the cubs after they arrived at Londolozi.*
**Bottom right:** *Hunting laundry in the camp.*

**Top left:** *The perfect spot for a catnap – between the flysheet and the tent roof in camp.*
**Above left:** *Play fighting on the sandbank at T'Ingwe Island, Zambia.*
**Above right:** *Little Girl reaches for the frisbee in a spectacular leap.*
**Far right:** *Little Boy, always the clown, performs a cheeky move during a soccer game.*

Top left: Jumping practice.
Left: Even at six months, Little Boy displays the intimidating ferocity of a leopard defending its meat.
Above: The classic cool gaze of the leopard emerges, even in cubhood.
Right: Little Boy interprets the scent deposited by a passing leopard – one of the ways in which leopards communicate with one another.

*Left:* Elmon bonds with Little Boy and Little Girl soon after their arrival at Londolozi.
*Right:* Skillful tree climbing is part of a leopard's education.
*Below:* Snooping down a warthog hole can be risky, but Little Girl's curiosity gets the better of her.
*Next page:* Coming down is often more difficult than going up.

# CHAPTER THREE

# *Kunjani?*

*How are you?*

Early the next morning, in the grey light of pre-dawn, we all gathered around the wire mesh of the boma, peering through the shadows. Our concern was met with an absolute silence. There was neither sight nor sound of the cubs, not even the slightest hiss or scurry to reassure us.

The previous evening, when we took them into their boma, the straw lining of their travelling box was soiled and wet with urine. We were worried about the cubs' comfort and dignity, but were unsure how to replace the straw without distressing them further. In the wild, a leopard mother keeps her cubs meticulously clean and moves them at regular intervals from one den-site to another. This prevents the build-up of parasites and of the telltale scents that alert rival predators such as lion or hyena. But it is about more than survival. Her immaculate cleanliness also imparts to her cubs at an early age the dignity that is key to a cat's sense of self.

After some discussion we provided an optional box for the cubs, which we hoped would appeal to their curiosity and so lure them out of the dirty one. We placed a slightly larger cardboard box, comfortably lined with fresh grass, adjacent to their green box, thinking that while the cubs might feel vulnerable in the sudden openness of the boma, they might find the cardboard box less threatening, even interesting. It might work as a halfway house between their box and the boma.

We all volunteered to take our sleeping bags into the boma, to sleep there on the sandy floor and offer our bodies as comfort to the cubs during their first night without their mother, surrounded as they were by the unfamiliar sounds and scents of the wilderness. But we reckoned our gesture would be counterproductive so we withdrew to our tents, leaving the cubs in their boma, all of us glancing anxiously over our shoulders as we walked away. As an afterthought, I took a pink blanket off one of the camp beds and draped it over the two boxes. At least it might protect them from the chill autumn wind. In a natural den-site, the cubs would be hidden in a fairly tight space. I reckoned that if they felt contained, as they would in the secrecy of a den somewhere in a root system or the recesses of some fallen rock, then hopefully they would feel less afraid when the tormenting cackles of hyena cut through the darkness of the night.

I didn't sleep much that night. The intense contact with the leopard cubs had left me with a sense of acceleration in my whole being. I lay awake wondering what was going through the cubs' minds. I tried to imagine how bombarded their senses were and how deep their feeling of dislocation must be if I, who could put a name to what was happening, felt as disoriented as I did.

In this half-sleeping, half-waking state, my mind spun with the possibilities of what lay ahead. Images of Mother Leopard loomed in my dreams, growing larger and then receding, at once vague and ill-defined, then becoming unnaturally bright and focused. I slept fitfully, often waking with a start, anxious for the cubs. I tried to send them as much reassurance as I could.

My thoughts turned to their birth mother in her cage in Zimbabwe. I knew she would be calling for her cubs, low soft moans as she searched everywhere. She would call in this way for a few days and then, not finding them, cease looking. In captivity, cubs are removed from their mothers at this age, whatever their future is to be. When hand-raised, cubs are more tractable. As I lay thinking of her, pale rays of moonlight slanted through the window of my tent. Even though the cubs' mother was thousands of kilometres away, it was the same moonlight that would be shining through the bars of her cage, throwing striped shadows across the floor as she paced up and down. Would she be comforted if she knew that though her life had been spent in captivity, the two precious cubs she had lost that day would in time be wild and free? Was there any way of her knowing that her cubs were to participate in the work of telling the story of the leopard in a film that could help to restore right relations between humans and leopards?

In the early hours of the morning the wind settled, and in the stillness that followed all life listened and waited for something to happen. Then, gradually the sounds of the bush restored harmony, creating an ease within me. A Skops owl hooted its hauntingly beautiful song and was answered faithfully by its mate from beyond the donga. A lioness grunted low and soft, relocating with her sisters from her pride. Would these living sounds of the night touch the cubs and reach something deep and instinctive within them?

As we stood trying to make out where the cubs were in their boma, I saw that they had pulled their blanket to the ground and dragged the corner of it into their green box, leaving the bulk of it fanned out over the sandy floor of the boma. There, entwined in each other's arms in the folds of the incongruous pink blanket, lay the cubs, snuggled up to it as if it were fur. I swallowed hard at the poignancy of the scene. These two creatures, not yet eight weeks old and weighing less than two kilograms, were trying to take care of themselves. It spoke of their need for comfort and nurturing and of their courage. My throat tightened and for the first time I felt a cold flicker of doubt. Could we actually do this? I had been so confident of being able to take leopard cubs to a life of freedom, but what if they rejected us and our offer of assistance?

The presence of the cubs altered the tone in the camp from eagerness to subdued awe. Before their arrival the previous evening, the camp had been noisy and chaotic, filled with the sounds of preparation and anticipation. Then, as soon as the cubs arrived, a cautious silence descended, something like the hush of respect reserved for sacred places. We moved around treading lightly, whispering to one another. As we sat around the campfire that evening, an enamel coffee mug fell from the table to the concrete slab on the ground. The clatter it caused was so dissonant that all of us leapt to our feet as one to retrieve it in our eagerness to smooth over the situation. In some ways we felt like new parents, wanting to check constantly that the baby was still breathing. In another way, we were initiates standing at the edge of a great mystery, our uncertainty reflecting the awe we felt in the presence of the cubs. The reality of their wildness was so stark: the scent of them, their electric energy, their purity.

I was acutely aware of the delicacy of the moment, concerned that nothing should shatter the fragility of these vital first encounters. Everything that happened between us now would lay the foundations for the relationship we hoped to build with the cubs.

It was a time to stand back and take our cue from the cubs. They had endured the most stressful event of their lives, separation from their mother and transition into the care of a group of humans, a shattering experience surrounded by rapidly changing environmental stimuli. Would the cubs cope with the rate and intensity of these changes? What they needed most of all was a period of unchanging calm to allow them a sense of control over their own fate – no matter how small – for choice is the basis of freedom for a wild animal. The cubs needed to be alone to analyse their new situation, to take in all the sights and smells around them in their own time and to give some form to their perceptions, to realise that the 'danger' they had faced was over. Most important for their self-confidence was for them to realise that, in one way or another, they had triumphed over it.

As we expected, the food in the boma lay untouched. This would be the case for a couple of days until the cubs' focus on defence broadened to one of adaptation. As their stress subsided, their appetites would return.

On our first day together we simply introduced ourselves to the cubs, each of our team taking turns to sit for a brief period at the far end of their boma and present ourselves. But for a long while, not even their instinctive curiosity would entice them from the safety of the dark corners of the travelling box, which had become their refuge.

When it was my turn I sat very still, making no sound and feigning as much disinterest as I could, as is the way of cats. Gradually, the cubs' curiosity got the better of them and they tentatively poked their heads out of the box, sniffing gingerly at what lay around them while eyeing me suspiciously. Then, keeping my body low to the ground and not looking directly into their eyes so as to appear less confrontational, I edged across the sand floor and positioned myself closer, allowing the details of who I was, how I smelt and what form my energy took to reach them.

As the first cub stepped cautiously forward, twitching its nose to catch my scent, I took it gently and held it by the scruff of the neck. From the slighter size of its body I knew it was the female. Holding a cub by the scruff of the neck induces a state of tonic immobility, a complete flaccidity of the muscles that allows a mother cat to carry her cubs safely in her mouth without injury. Working with her involuntary compliance, I held the little creature against my body as I had done instinctively in response to the male cub's cries of distress on the airstrip the previous day. The exchange between us in that brief moment of holding had communicated beyond the actual gesture and across the barrier of species. I hoped to re-establish the connection, this time with the female. Even though I was uncertain exactly what the experience meant to the cub, I trusted that the eloquent language of touch would convey my goodwill.

After a brief moment, I repositioned my hand under her belly with my fingers spread wide, holding her firmly under the chest to create the feeling of being held hammock-like with her head and limbs unconfined. This way of holding young animals allows them a feeling of freedom and security. It is also a good way to avoid being bitten and scratched but it must be done firmly, as hesitation is sensed immediately and will be quickly outmanoeuvred.

She allowed this. Then I placed her on the ground a short distance from the box. She froze momentarily, holding her body low to the ground, then dashed back into the box.

Silence.

Her brother came out to investigate and gave me the same opportunity. He too bolted for cover when I set him down. Perhaps some fear was released in the touching, for he emerged a short while later and sat at a safe distance from the box, staring at me with startled curiosity. His sister remained defiant and unforgiving, staying in the box and growling for some time. Then she too emerged and sat blinking in the light, holding back slightly behind her brother's shoulder. Both of them tolerated my presence, seemingly ignoring me, but sending the occasional furtive glance my way.

On the second day we took shifts, lying on the ground of the boma in a non-threatening posture and allowing the cubs to size us up. The young female cub continued hissing, spitting and growling defensively while mostly hiding in the box. But the young male was into exploring and took tentative steps forward, gradually increasing his distance from the box before dashing back in again when his courage failed him.

On the third day the cubs came out of the box and edged around the boma, sniffing, although their knees were bent and bodies taut with readiness to run. Surprisingly, the young female was showing some willingness to feed. On standby was a baby's bottle containing a mixture of infant formula with vitamins and mineral additives, enriched with dollops of cream.

Knowing she would back off if anything moved too close towards her, I flicked a few drops of the liquid, allowing them to fall on her nose. Offended, she drew back sharply, shook her head vigorously and then tried to lick it off. Her dawning recognition that this new irritation was food, was comical. She latched onto the bottle with urgency, feeding hungrily on the milk while her blazing eyes and the reversing motion of her body, paws dug defiantly in the sand, indicated her ongoing mistrust.

After feeding, both cubs were calmer. They even began to play tentatively with one another. We were elated. It is heartwarming to see a young creature feed with a healthy appetite. We had established a vital connection. This defined our status with the cubs. We could provide food.

After initial familiarisation, we worked towards establishing a physical bridge using deliberate touch, a kind of body talk. We started with long, slow movements with the back of our hands along their flanks whenever they passed us. We hoped this might prove to be a poignant reminder of their mother grooming them at birth.

The cubs' response was ambiguous. Our touch was pleasurable to them, perhaps evoking fond memories, but our energies must have felt so different and this confused them. Often they would twitch and shake as if an electric shock was passing between us.

In the 1950s, some cruel but revealing research was done on the psychological implications of physical contact. This remains the basis for theories on bonding. The Harlow experiments showed that baby monkeys that were deprived of their mothers, more often than not chose the physical comfort of contact over food. Knowledge of this underpinned our instinctive response to mother these babies, for that is what they were.

By now the cubs were walking freely in the boma, mostly giving us a wide berth. They still had the choice between hiding in their box, or venturing out to investigate the humans whose presence was now a constant. The temptation to play with them was overwhelming, an urge we had to subdue. The wildness that ruled their spirits would fear this premature familiarity. Frequent outbreaks of hissing and spitting reminded us that we were not entirely welcome, but we persisted in initiating contact in as non-threatening a manner as we could. Leaving them isolated in their boma was not an option. For us to be effective guardians, we needed to create a relationship. They in turn needed to imprint on us and identify us not only as the source of their food. They needed to understand that they were safe with us.

We had not chosen names for the cubs, as we hoped that names would suggest themselves as we grew to know each other. But nothing that any of us came up with stuck, or seemed to belong to them in any way. It was as if these creatures touched us in a way that could not be verbalised. On a practical level though, we needed to refer to them in some way.

I noticed our Shangaan workers referring to the cubs as 'the little boy' and 'the little girl'. There was something quaint and endearing in the way they had translated the gender definitions. So the cubs became known as 'Little Boy' and 'Little Girl'.

I think the cubs liked the names too, 'b' and 'g' being good, strong sounds which caught their attention. In my heart I thought of them as my little brother and sister. Coincidentally, I noticed JV referring to them in this way too when he was talking to them privately. There was something symmetrical in seeing them as family which enhanced the significance of Mother Leopard. After all, it was she who had birthed in JV a lifelong fascination with Leopard and in me a shift in consciousness, which I only fully realised with hindsight.

We were impressed by the enormous power of the cubs' bodies and it was a joy to see them thrive. They began to eat voraciously and turned into round butterballs almost overnight. The ragged and stressed appearance of their arrival soon vanished, along with the watery look they had in their eyes. Their thick, woolly fur coats would disappear in a few months' time, making way for the sleek rosetted coats of adulthood. Their cub coat was long, thick and coarse with silken strands hinting at the future glossiness of their adult coats. This fur was mottled grey and fawn, dull to look at but an effective camouflage for young cubs hiding in their den in the wild.

Their ears were large and round and comically disproportionate to the rest of their bodies, suggesting how important hearing was to their survival at this stage. The ears were set low on their heads, revealing the powerful, dome-shaped skull, characteristic of the big cats. Inside their ears, the softest, white, down-like fur sprouted in great tufts. Like radar dishes they would swivel around constantly to catch and magnify all sound stimuli coming from their surroundings. You could almost see the cubs memorising the myriad data for future use.

Their whiskers were full, long and white. One of Little Boy's whiskers was kinked and hung over his eye at an engaging angle; another had a twirl to it. With maternal concern I tried to straighten them out and failing, hoped in time they would right themselves. There was no way he could ever look fierce as an adult with whiskers like that.

Cats' whiskers, or 'vibrissae', are embedded in a bundle of nerves connected to the brain by the same channel as the nerves for the eyes. This helps them to 'see' in the dark through a hypersensitivity to the subtle movements of air currents around objects. Whiskers are also expressive, moving as the muscles of their faces move to reveal their state of mind more articulately than any sounds could. We learned to read these emotions quickly on Little Girl's face, as she had an especially rich repertoire of expressions. In her early days with us, because she was annoyed, she frequently pursed her lips in irritation, sending the whiskers forward in a comical picture of primness.

Her eyes were mottled blue-grey. Beyond the distrust of us reflected there, was an expression of wisdom archaic in character, mirroring the depth and complexity of an old soul. Little Boy's eyes were flecked with green, suggesting for the future the topaz colour of such startling beauty found in some adult leopards. His expression – when it wasn't of puzzlement or curiosity at the goings-on around him – was one of good-natured congeniality.

The cubs' bodies were typically kittenish, with rounded tummies, their legs squat and stubby. They would remain proportionately short as their bodies grew, creating the low centre of gravity that makes leopards so agile in trees. It was hard to imagine how one day their spiky tails would develop into the lavish, muscular tails which the adult leopard holds with such grace as a counter-balance in trees, or uses it as a rudder in a chase. The cubs' paws were overly large, as in most young creatures. They would have to grow into them. Their needle-like claws could scratch painfully and we had to accept that if we wanted to engage with the cubs at all, we would have to live with wounds. Until they learnt the skill of retracting their claws, a large bottle of Betadine antiseptic stood on standby.

The cubs' milk teeth were all through, and the little canines could rip quite destructively, hinting at the power of the lethal canines that would replace them. Little Girl showed some unpleasant biting behaviour, although her brother seldom bit. Usually in small animals this reaction is more about fear than aggression.

Above the whisker line on their faces was the identifying pattern of spots, the configuration as unique to each leopard as a fingerprint is to a human being. Little Girl had three spots on the right, two on the left; Little Boy, two on the left, two on the right, details which we registered in the data we kept. This spot pattern would never change in their lifetime and could be used to identify them, no matter how our paths diverged.

The daily ritual of grooming formed a vital part of our attempts to connect with the cubs. They fiercely resisted being washed and our efforts were confounded by our clumsiness and strangeness. In her efficiency, a leopard mother pins her wriggly cub down firmly with her paw to wash its face. We couldn't have pinned our cubs down even if we tried. Their enormous power, driven by their desire to wrestle free and their sheer squirmability, prevented it. So we took a rough towel, dampened it and dabbed at their faces – a hit and miss affair – to mimic what their mother would do to remove the residue of food smudged there during feeding. Washing prevents parasites from accumulating and encourages the cubs into their own grooming rituals, a part of any cat's etiquette. It was also a gesture fundamental to our bonding.

Karin and I took special delight in the washing sessions. Perhaps it was the youthful resistance that amused us so much and touched our maternal instincts. Little Girl's face was so expressive, her eyes flashing indignantly as we tried to clean her. Little Boy was always tolerant of what came his way, even though he initially resisted having his face washed with distaste. When we insisted, he would lower his eyelids halfway and look sideways, wrinkling his nose and swivelling his ears back, all these gestures combining in an expression of great long-suffering.

At the end of the first week, with the cubs looking relaxed and moving comfortably in their boma, we felt confident enough to take them from the camp down to the donga – the doorway to their wilderness playground. For now, as their mother would have done, we carried the cubs by the scruff of their necks, and for extra security supported them firmly under their bottoms. When we set them down they froze instinctively, then crouched in preparation to run. After a few seconds of silence, as if watching magic at work, the tension released itself from their bodies. They could feel the living energy of the earth in the sand, the grass and the rough spiky feel of thorn beneath their paws.

Morning was breaking and as the sun rose, the air warmed. Insects came alive and the birds began their song. A black-headed oriole called in its liquid notes and then, seeing us, sounded its charring alarm. The cubs, as if remembering something long-forgotten, responded to the subliminal embrace of Nature and began to explore.

Little Boy was the first. He began to bat at a twig lying next to him with his overly large paws, at first hesitantly and then with growing enthusiasm, as it began to spin around in friendly response.

After a moment of assessment, Little Girl began to move around, her nose twitching. During her exploration she discovered a tree. It was a russet bush willow, its long slender branches drooping low, twigs laden with bunches of coppery-brown, winged seeds which clattered in response to her nudging. She paused next to the tree, sensing the presence of life within it, then stood for a moment concentrating, as one trying to absorb an invisible message. The size of the tree fascinated her. She cocked her head this way and that and then looked upwards, blinking, following the reach of the trunk into the sky. Otherwise she stood perfectly still, absorbing all the information that was being offered.

Eventually she fell to investigating the more immediate details of the tree, sniffing at the patchy grey bark and tapping at it lightly with her paw. She struck it more firmly, sinking her tiny claws into it, then withdrew shyly, sat back and watched and waited for some reaction from the tree. It was as if she had found something she recognised as having life within it; so apparent was her expectation that it would respond.

Encouraged, I watched the two young leopards sitting on the floor of the dry river bed, dwarfed by the riverine trees and the granite boulders that towered over them. So fragile and vulnerable. Yet inherent in this picture was the notion of them taking their first steps towards life in the wild.

There was no resistant crouching when we returned the cubs to their boma, rather a joyful reaction to finding themselves in a familiar environment, a slight skip and acceleration to their step as they ran forward. They had come to recognise and accept that their boma, and not the travelling box, was their place of safety now.

That evening we offered the cubs fresh impala meat before their milk feed. They tore into it, eyes blazing, their canines ripping at it, swallowing whole bits in gulps, and then looked up expectantly for more. Young leopards suckle until they are about three months old, but at six weeks a leopard mother will take her cubs to her kills. For the following six-week period, until they are fully weaned, they feed on a very rich diet of both her milk and meat. We were imitating this pattern.

The cubs chewed at the rubber teats of their feeding bottles, suggesting they were ready to move from sucking to lapping. So we gave them their milk feed in a saucer, hoping also to reduce the number of teats they were destroying.

The bottle feed began with the cubs sucking comfortably, but with their impatience to gulp the milk down it would deteriorate rapidly into a chewing and tugging exercise. The inevitable deluge of milk which followed as the teat tore suddenly and soaked their faces, left Little Girl frightened, her fur spiky and dripping. She glared at us in blame. Everyone seemed unnerved by the experience.

Little Boy didn't mind being drenched. Having food all over him was an unexpected bonus for one with his appetite. Perhaps because he could swallow bigger quantities and feed faster than his sister, it was he who was the first to get the lapping motion right.

To begin with, Little Girl tapped at the milk in the saucer with her paw and then, watching her brother bending over it, copied him and submerged her nose in the milk. She tried to suckle from the saucer and inhaled the milk up her nose. Coughing and spluttering she fled from the saucer, rubbing her nose with her paw, her expression hostile and suspicious.

A tension began to develop between the cubs when they were eating meat that was not evident when they were feeding on milk. There were low, threatening growls from Little Boy. Little Girl became scared and grumpy. With his superior size and strength, Little Boy was actively preventing her from getting at the meat.

What would a mother leopard have done? She would probably have allowed a certain amount of competition between the cubs to strengthen their resolve – for them to become aware that feeding involved competition, such as being smarter, if not stronger.

Little Girl, with her highly-strung nature, became even more nervous and cowed. Providing extra food didn't help. Little Boy pirated Little Girl's share no matter how much meat there was. He sat jealously guarding his booty, simultaneously growling and gulping as fast as he could.

In the end we separated the cubs during meals. This caused Little Girl a different kind of stress. She left her food untouched and climbed up the tree in the boma, calling anxiously to locate her brother. Little Boy didn't miss a beat. His attention went where the food went.

We took the cubs down to the donga again soon after that. The recognition of familiar territory was instant. This was the way we planned to allow their world to expand – by building on the confidence which familiarity gave them. Little Girl went directly to the red bush willow tree that so fascinated her on the previous visit. Once again she sat looking at it with concentrated awareness. Little Boy took up batting at small twigs and branches lying on the sandy floor. Then he experimented with scurrying in and out of clumps of grass to see if he could escape from himself. The moment took him and soon he was spinning in circles after his own tail, pausing now and then, his eyes darting back and forth to see where it had escaped to.

There was an alertness in the cubs that showed in their body language as a tautness – but it was not the same tension of muscle as when they had arrived and were fearful of us. Now it was more an eagerness expressed in their stance as they waited for the games that nature presented to them – leaves swept across the donga, grasses blowing in the breeze or twigs that spun and flipped in response to their playful paws.

The donga was a living laboratory where the cubs could play and explore, investigate and learn from Nature – the only teacher apart from their mother who could educate them. In this natural environment, the cubs would learn about the simple laws that governed their physical existence. Going up a tree meant having to come down. Some creatures could be chased. Others chased you. Here they were exposed to the constantly changing experience offered by various inhabitants of the bush, from grasshoppers and frogs to tortoises and birds, the impala that danced across the sand on delicate legs, to the elephants that followed the course of the donga system in the dry winter months, seeking the last remaining green grasses of the riverine vegetation.

And then there were the predators. Here in the donga, the cubs would come to understand the linkages and flow of the natural world. They would learn about the dynamics of Nature's subtler energies – the essence of other life forms – the rocks and the grasses, the wind and the trees – those the Shamans call the 'devic' or nature spirits.

The more sensory stimulation Little Boy and Little Girl received, the more developed their minds could become and the better their edge in coping with the unexpected. Sensory stimulation causes nerve cells in the brain to grow and make new synaptic connections with other nerve cells. This network expands to accommodate and accumulate new information.

But how were we to stimulate the cubs' senses in the absence of their mother? For lack of a better idea, we did a human thing and gave the cubs two soft toys. One was a stuffed, felt lion. The way he was sewn together gave him a comical expression of surprise. The other was a leopard cub, a fluffy toy with emerald green buttons for eyes and a red, woollen nose.

Both toys were bigger than the cubs, but they pounced on them without hesitation. Growling menacingly, they sank their needle teeth and claws into the toys, 'killed' them and dragged them around the boma, in a virtuoso display of dominance.

We hung 'Lion' from a string and he became a punching bag, with both cubs rising up on their hind legs and cuffing at him like boxers with their front paws. 'Leppie's' role was to be dragged around. He was left lying on the ground, taken to various spots around the camp and without fail, into the sleeping box in the boma at night. The cubs bit into his neck and then dragged him off between their splayed front paws as if he were a carcass. Their neck and shoulder muscles were taught with the effort of holding him, chin drawn in firmly, in a miniature version of the way an adult leopard drags around its kill before hoisting it into a tree. Leppie was killed and dragged endlessly, but the cubs never made any attempt to eat him. We couldn't have chosen better toys to nurture the cubs' sense of mastery.

It may have been the soft toys that stimulated it, for strategic play fighting began in earnest between the cubs around this time. Despite their weight difference and Little Boy's dominance over meat, the cubs were equally matched. Little Girl countered her brother's strengths with her lightning ability to analyse and strategise, quickly learning her way around her brother. In their play they expressed their unique characters. While Little Boy would run directly at his sister, hoping to topple her with the power of his chest and the weight of his body, Little Girl used her wits. She initiated a tackle by launching herself at her brother in the direct style of attack he understood. Then, when he thought he had mastery, she feigned withdrawal from the fray. Little Boy, open and straightforward by nature and innocently obedient to the rules of the game, would relax his counter-attack, thinking he was victorious. Just as he was righting himself to claim his moment, Little Girl wheeled around and leapt at him from an oblique angle, laying him flat. Right in these early stages, she was the superior tactician.

Along with this high-spiritedness, the cubs began to vocalise. At first it was with squeaks and growls in the play-fighting, expressing the limits of their tolerance to each other's bites and tackles. As we began to recognise the different calls they produced, we tried to respond appropriately, hoping to indicate to them by our reactions that we were receptive to whatever it was they were communicating.

Vocalisation in leopards deals mostly with basic, survival-linked issues: 'Here I am', 'Where are you?', 'I am hungry', 'Back off'. The more complex, subtler messages are relayed through body talk – an eloquent expression of eyes, ears, tails, distance or proximity and full body posture, either individually or in combination – and mind talk.

The first call to us from the cubs that signalled 'approach' after days of 'back off' hisses was a high-pitched yowl, filled with urgency. We called it 'the food noise'. It's a cry which is universal and which touches every mother in a deep, instinctual place. There is a tone to the call that short-circuits everything else from her mind and drives her to satisfy the hunger of her young. As surrogate parents we reacted the same way. Appetite is the surest indicator of the physical health of an animal.

They began to make another interesting approach sound – a puffing noise something like the chuffing tigers make in greeting. When I first heard Little Boy puffing, I looked at him and read clear expectation in his body talk. I wondered if he was trying to relocate his sister and then, with

Kunjani?

a lurching feeling of sadness, I realised that was not it. She was quite clearly within his sight. Little Boy was trying to find his mother.

We picked up on the puffing sound, repeating it and responding to it strictly when the cubs indicated it was appropriate. In vocalising this way, we hoped the cubs would transfer to us whatever the communication had been with their mother. They made the sound when we moved out of sight and rejoined them or when we saw them for the first time in the day. We must have been getting it right, because there was instant alertness in their bodies when we puffed. The cubs would swing their heads around to locate us. It was a joy to have woven another thread of connection between us even in this simple way. Yet for a while after, I thought I detected remnants of hope that their mother may have returned. From the expectant look I read in their eyes, I realised that we had a long way to go before the cubs accepted us as their adoptive parents.

There was no way of ever really knowing how the cubs had experienced what for me were emotionally tender spots – suddenly their mother was gone; then there were humans. In a moment of fear or confusion, who could they turn to?

Were we to brush past these moments, relying on the adaptability of the young cats to carry them through? I ended up using a technique I improvised and stuck to for the duration of our time with Little Boy and Little Girl. I cleared my mind of all else, allowing only the moment to flow as simply as I could. I hoped that the seed thought would translate into paralanguage – body talk, ESP, subtle changes in my energy field, some non-verbal communication beyond my knowledge – and that the cubs might sense my empathy. I could think of no other way to reassure them. My special interest was communication. After all, what if this worked?

Leopards are territorial animals. Their social system is regulated by this imperative. Within their home range, they reserve certain rights including those of hunting, mating and breeding and will aggressively contest any would-be intruder who fails to observe territorial etiquette. It was too early in the cubs' development for them to exercise any such claims, but we could start nurturing the instinct with some foundation work, simulating the experiences the cubs would have in the wild.

They would have begun to follow their mother within her home range to her kills from about six weeks old, leaving the relative safety of their den. Encounters as nature presented them would have taught them about

41

territory. On these forays at their mother's side they would have learnt how crucial perfect knowledge of their home range is.

In our walking to and from the donga, we lay down a map of retreat from any danger the cubs might encounter. The more familiar they became with the finest detail of every bush or tree, every twist in the path, the safer they would be under attack. They would know in advance which trees could receive them in flight, where crevices lay in which they could hide, which ground surface would give them better traction or which angle gave them the shortcut home. This would give them the edge in a life-or-death chase. It needed to become second nature to them.

A leopard receives news of its world by reading the language of Nature, from the visual cues of broken branches or droppings deposited and from the various scents laid by passers-by. By listening for the proximity or distance of calls and analysing the messages, the leopard updates its information on how the land lies, who is visiting or has passed through. Constant checking out of these discreet signals helps them avoid unexpected confrontation.

Intimate knowledge of the landscape frees up the perceptions from the energy-consuming work of continually examining every detail, into the less mentally demanding mode of monitoring. Only that which is out of place, that which disturbs, that which is unfamiliar, needs to be attended to.

In imitation of Nature's way, we walked with the cubs at daybreak and then again in the late afternoon at dusk. At these times the cubs' energy would rise in a pattern that is the natural behaviour of leopards. As nocturnal creatures, they conserve their energies during the heat of the day and hunt under the cover of dark at night, or at dawn when their powers peak and their sensory abilities are most acute. They hunt at the optimum time and patrol their territory to read the signs that inform them of potential danger or opportunity.

But there is more to territorial patrol than survival. There is also a psychological benefit – the sense of security that comes from belonging to an organised system with a recognisable routine. Nature's expressions present themselves in patterns that repeat themselves into rhythms, the cycle of the seasons, day and night. Perhaps what provides comfort is a resonance in the psyche of the first rhythm we know – the beating of our mother's heart.

If we were to assist in turning the cubs' fragile sense of self into something more sturdy, mastery over their small universe would go a long way to developing their self-esteem. We could see this process working within the cubs. In the beginning they were scared of everything that moved. Now they were confident in the familiar surrounds of their 'territory' around the camp and the donga.

The radius of our walks from T'Ingwe camp was small to begin with. Even so, the cubs often needed to interrupt the adventure with a quick nap. There were times too when they would be distracted from the serious business of territorial patrol by a birdsong, or a butterfly's flight pattern. Little Girl developed her own ritual of communing with the russet bush willow tree whenever we passed by. Both cubs were fascinated by the dung of other animals. Their noses twitched eagerly as they interpreted the story it told them and they stored the memory of its scent. Often the excitement and stimulation of our walks would wear them out completely and their legs couldn't manage the return trip. Then we'd carry them back home, as their mother would have done.

As the days went by, the cubs anticipated their walks and waited eagerly at the door of their boma. Any reluctance or lack of interest alerted us quickly to an upset tummy or a bad mood. These outings were great fun. The walks gave the cubs more clues about our relationship with them. Although we continued to sit with them in their boma, those visits were more about mutual discovery of who we were as individuals. Walks into the donga were different – a shared adventure, an activity we did together. A most unlikely family – a group of humans and two leopard cubs. Exploring in the bush bonded us.

In the cool of the autumn morning mist floated from the dank undergrowth, bringing an ethereal quality to the atmosphere of the woodlands and fields. The cubs found the freshness energising and became mischievous with their heightened levels of energy. They initiated all sorts of games, at first with each other and then, as trust developed, they invited us to participate in games of stalk-and-pounce.

Ambush was a big favorite with Little Boy. Hiding in wait for his quarry was about as secretive as he could be. His fledgling skills at concealment were hilarious. He crouched down behind a single tuft of grass with his bottom in the air, every part of him plainly visible except the portion of his head between his eyes and nose. But Little Boy believed he was out of sight and so out of sight he was. We played along, humouring him, pretending not to see him although his tail was flying like a mast in the air. He was so delighted by his success as he made a terrifying leap into the air, attaching himself to our calves or ankles, that the pretence was worth it. The scratches from his needle-like claws were painful, but Little Boy's delight in the victory of his assaults and his growing sense of himself as a powerful leopard were too endearing to deny.

How best to begin work with the cubs? Before their release, they were to act in a feature film – the story of Mother Leopard. We needed to introduce them to cameras. Filming from the back of a vehicle had shown us how sensitive wild animals are to the presence of a long lens. Clearly, there was an added intensity to the feeling of being watched when the 'eye' was as large and staring as the lenses we used. We let the cubs sniff around the cameras and bat at their reflections, gently desensitising them to being looked at through the lens. After several trials in the familiarity of their 'territory', we were ready to take them off on their first official film shoot. We were concerned that their early experience of the green box might have traumatised them, yet they seemed quite happy about their new travelling cages. We laid the boxes next to one another in the back of the film vehicle, secured them fast and went bumping off down the dirt track. There was no sound of protest coming from the cubs.

We headed for a higher-lying area of Londolozi known as Nyamakunzi Crest, named after a black-maned lion that used to reign there. Not far from the crest is a rough outcrop of granite boulders. Mother Leopard used this den site for several of her litters. By the way they had fallen, the rocks had created hiding places in the shape of crevices and clefts. Clumps of titawa thorn protruded, making access to its secret parts tricky.

We put the cubs down next to the boulders to let them feel their way around. Both of them froze for a moment or two, going down on their haunches in preparation to run. Then, after nothing terrible seemed to happen, they felt confident enough to explore.

As soon as they felt the sturdiness of the granite rocks beneath their feet and discovered the crevices, there was that same visible release of tension in their bodies. They played among the rocks, hiding and pressing themselves into the slightest cracks, practising their skills of concealment and seeing just how far they could creep into the fractures of the rocks. They tested the width of the gap with their head and whiskers, assessing whether the rest of their bodies could follow. Being in the dark recesses of tiny caves was new to the cubs, but they took to it as if it was a homecoming. They played with ease, moving with agility. Even their round tummies and wobbly legs seemed graceful as they darted in and out of the crevices. Their eyes were bright, filled with excitement as their pupils dilated with the thrill of the adventure.

To facilitate filming we took a container of chopped meat along. Could we lure the cubs into position by placing small pieces where we wanted them to be and then letting them use their own initiative as to what they did next? Could we work in this way, following them in what they did spontaneously rather than pressing them to perform a rehearsed routine – the conventional method of filming trained animals? This impromptu technique worked well, and so we kept it in mind for the main feature film shoot when the cubs would be six months old.

Those who had worked with leopards in captivity or with animals trained for film work advised us to separate Little Boy and Little Girl into individual bomas in the camp. If the cubs were separated while they were young and impressionable, they would imprint on us rather than on each other, thereby making them more tractable and easier to work with. The notion sat uncomfortably with us. It fell firmly within the paradigm of human convenience and dominance over animals.

Our guiding principle was based on what would best assist the cubs in their reintegration into the wild. What they could learn from one another in play, what they shared by being together, far outweighed the short-term needs of our film. So Little Boy and Little Girl stayed together.

In their own way, the cubs had shown us clearly that day at Titawa Rocks just how to get the best from them on film. We would reflect the natural charm of uncontrived situations. It was the way Mother Leopard had allowed JV to film her daily activities that created the magic they shared.

Our role on our dusk and dawn walking ritual was one of guardianship. It was all too easy to be drawn into the wonder of the cubs' explorations and to watch them unfolding like flowers, minute by minute. Yet potential danger was everywhere. It could swoop from above in the shape of a raptor or strike as a python hidden in the crevices of the rock. The cubs had no actual experience of any of these threats. Their knowledge about survival, that knowledge we call instinct, needed to be activated by circumstances and honed by practice.

The donga had been the core of Mother Leopard's home range. As far as we knew, after her death a territorial vacuum had been created there. It was only a matter of time before another female leopard would probe the territory. We were on the alert for any signs. All predators are aggressive and kill the young of other predators. A rival predator opportunistically coursing through the grassland; an hyena in its uncanny way of sniffing out food; the territorial male leopard that roamed the wider range encompassing the females' smaller territories; the pride of lions which included the donga in their territory – all of these were potential dangers to the cubs.

We were armed with rifles on our walks. There is seldom wanton aggression in Nature. Aggression from animals in the bush usually results from the clumsiness of people moving too close to an animal, evoking a defence. When confronted by a wild animal, it is usually best to retreat, to crouch low to the ground, lowering one's threatening human profile, to conceal oneself if possible and in every way indicate appeasement and the intention to withdraw. If the situation is too fraught or too far-gone, bluffing about one's size and capability by making big, threatening gestures or a loud aggressive noise may be an option – especially with cats. This is, of course, total chicanery, and the deafening crash of a rifle shot aimed high in the air adds to the effectiveness of the pantomime. Arm-waving and shouting might startle a lion should we chance upon one, but once he became aware of the cubs at our sides, nothing would stop him from attacking and killing them if he wanted to.

Walking in the wilderness demands an unwavering focus on the present. It is so easy with human artifice to allow our attention to wander backwards and forwards in time. For such mental freedom in the wild you first have to ensure your physical safety as a leopard does by climbing high into the trees, before allowing its mind to roam.

With repeated practice, my concentration improved. I found my eyesight sharpening, my hearing skills becoming more acute and experienced a growing skill of noticing that which was out of place. For me, this was a new way of perceiving sensory information. I discovered that these skills could be trained and as they grew, new ways of using them became apparent. There was a simple way of isolating senses. By focusing my consciousness on hearing, to the exclusion of the other senses, more sensitivity to sound became available. If I soft-focused my vision, not looking at any object in particular, but rather taking in a general visual spread, I noticed the slightest movement more easily than if I deliberately looked for it.

I had to learn to intuit more acutely, to sense from what was apparent, what might lie beyond. Relying on my intuition became critical, not only for the cubs' survival, but for my own. It was invigorating to expand into these untapped aspects of myself, to find myself participating so actively in the life of the wilderness.

I began to see a glimmer of what the greater experience of living with these leopard cubs meant. They had drawn me into this vital and alive state. They were teaching and leading me as much as I was assisting in their defence and education. The sense of symmetry in this curious exchange led me to spend many hours wondering about the deeper, spiritual meaning of our relationship with Little Boy and Little Girl, beyond the linear, narrative experience of our days together.

Mythologies talk of a state or a time where there was no barrier between species, and teach that the divine reveals itself in Nature. For me, the most mystical aspect of our time with the cubs was the relationship between us. I wondered what we could offer each other, how we could complement the other's life and spiritual experience.

I believe that there are collective as well as personal reasons for the soul choices we make. I wondered what the birth vision of these two leopard cubs was. What had they chosen to learn during this incarnation on earth? Were they seeking to learn about humans on behalf of the collective mind of leopards? How could I most properly assist in the process? What did Little Boy and Little Girl need to know about human intention? About me? There were times with the cubs when it felt there was no differentiation of species. We were just beings. Then there were times when a self-consciousness would creep between us and one or the other would reverse behind the barrier.

I needed to create an openness within myself, to be receptive. I needed to set aside assumptions to be free of projection. In the quiet moments sitting in the boma with the cubs, I found myself filled with reverence for the purity of their wildness. Complete obedience to the laws of their species and to the greater universal laws is so unquestioned in wild animals. Carl Jung called them 'the priests of God'. There was something holy about the cubs. I was humbled. At moments like these, I felt a sadness that I couldn't fathom, something close to nostalgia, of something that spoke of a time long ago. Something that was essentially lost to me.

As I visited the cubs, I began to have an uncanny sense that their reluctance, born of a fear of humans so ancient that it spoke to them from the depth of their cell tissue, began to break down. There appeared once or twice to be a tentative opening of a window, allowing brief access. It closed as rapidly as it had opened. As the days and weeks wore on, I sensed a subtle change in the cubs' way of relating. There was a slight shift in their begrudging tolerance of us.

I understood that if we were going to gain any access to them at all, we were going to have to work hard for it, to demonstrate a constant commitment and an unfailing patience. I learnt from JV's time with Mother Leopard that nothing comes easily with leopards. The cubs' lack of disclosure was also bound up with leopards' social choice to walk a solitary path. There was a contradiction for them inherent in creating any form of bonds. I thought that access would come from Little Boy first. Beneath the surface of Little Girl's acceptance of security and food, was a wide gulf of mistrust. I expected it would take a long time before she was prepared to give of herself or be genuinely interested in us.

Then one day, while sitting with the cubs, I lost concentration and my mind wandered. Gradually, I became aware that I was being watched. Out of the corner of my eye, I noticed Little Girl looking at me with an intensity I hadn't seen before. It was as though she was looking to find or understand something as her eyes searched my face. I didn't move or allow my thoughts to return to the immediate present, in case she sensed the shift and withdrew her enquiry.

Just then a scrub robin came flitting through the raisin bush outside the boma, singing its beautiful, full-throated song. In its simple exaltation, it always sounds to me like a hymn of joy. I was so captivated that I was able to allow Little Girl to pursue whatever it was she was up to. I didn't look at her directly, so there was no way of being sure whether or not she was planning to pounce at me. I concentrated on keeping my body language and energy field open. I focused on the song of the scrub robin.

Little Girl did not rush at me. She stayed as she was, half-concealed by a branch that lay between us, just looking at me. I understood that she was piecing together some curiosity about who I was that had stirred in her. It evoked in me the same feeling as when Mother Leopard had looked at us. As if she were not after any visual detail, she was scanning the image before her eyes, attuning herself to what lay beyond, rather than that which was apparent.

The moment held itself briefly. Then either Little Girl or I wavered, or both of us did. With exaggerated casualness, we each fell to our own displacement activities, she washing and me fiddling with a twig in the sand, as if to pretend that nothing had happened. But my heart knew that something important had passed between us. Something had changed.

There is play for joy and play for learning. Through play, Nature has provided a simple but ingenious education. The abundant energy and vigour the young are blessed with is focused directly on what is practical and what will ensure survival. During Little Boy and Little Girl's cubhood, skills laid down in their genetic memory needed to be released, made current and practised to perfection. Vigilance and patience had to be understood, timing perfected, stalking, pouncing and agility explored and individual limitations overcome. In their tree-tumbling games, their mock fighting and in their comic routine of ambush, the cubs were in training. In this play, every turn, every angle of approach expanded their repertoire and laid down a band of information in their neural patterning.

The cubs' sense of play called forth creativity as we invented new games to stretch their imagination. In play, the feeling of mastery that comes from small successes builds self-confidence and coping behaviour. The cubs learned how far they could go with each other. A special, high-pitched meow indicated their limits. Tension or anxiety was expressed symbolically and acted out, usually in an ambush attack on our ankles. We gauged from the cubs what novelty would excite them and extended games that they had initiated.

A gust of wind blew a wild date palm frond, used to make the garage roof in the camp, to the ground. Its rustling sound as its fronds waved tantalizingly in the breeze, was irresistible. Little Boy and Little Girl were on it like a flash, swiping and hooking at it, forcing it to react. Then, when it lay still, they rolled over and over the hard spine, lifting it, inviting another attack from its waving blades. We joined in, swinging the frond in a circle, encouraging the cubs to capture it. Little Girl soon worked out that if she cut through the bend, she'd have the tip of the palm frond in her paws before it swung full circle. Little Boy ran the full circle, convinced that he would triumph through that extra burst of speed. He was astonished to see his sister ahead of him. Little Boy needed to learn that life, like the palm leaf game, was about more than power – it was also about tactics and timing.

For most leopard cubs, jumping in trees is the best game ever. They learn which branches can support their weight and which are too slender. Little Boy's style was to rush into action and then see what the outcome was. He would run up a tree and launch himself at a branch. Inevitably, he would miscalculate and it would snap. Down he plunged, trying to recover his position by clinging to the slender branch with his powerful forearms. His bottom and hind legs would swing back and forth, toes reaching to find a grip, while he cast his eyes this way and that in desperation.

Little Girl always considered first. Then, drawing on her brother's calamities and former experience, she tested the branch with her foot before stepping onto it. She had her times of frivolity too when she abandoned herself to the fun of the tree game. The cubs made each other fall deliberately. The tumbling and the unpredictability of the ways of the branches challenged them. They learnt what size of branch could sustain their own weight. Leopards soon learn that though lions can climb trees, they are not as agile, nor can they climb as high as leopards can.

Falling from a tree can be dangerous, even fatal, despite leopards' tendency to land on their feet. A young Londolozi leopard called Stickanwayo, 'the one who walks with a stick', never fully recovered from tearing a ligament when she fell and hooked her leg on a branch. She walked with a dragging limp till the end of her life, which ended prematurely. Slowed down by her handicap, she was unable to escape from an hyena.

Everybody in the team came up with games. Elmon, in his direct way, quietly went off one day. We found him filling a mealie meal hessian bag with dry grass. Saying the cubs needed to learn to hold on, he strung the bag from a tamboti tree and swung it slightly. At first the cubs scampered under a bush, watching it suspiciously. Little Boy edged forward bravely, hissed at it then jumped back a few paces. Then his courage deserted him and he bolted, taking cover under a shrubby camphor bush. There he and Little Girl watched this strange creature that had suddenly appeared in the camp and altered the character of the tamboti tree – their tumbling tree – which they thought they knew so well.

After some time, curiosity got the better of Little Boy. He tapped at the straggling threads and then more confidently swiped at the bag itself, sending it swinging in the opposite direction. Little Girl, hiding behind his shoulder, applied her quick and lively mind to the problem. When the bag swung back at them, after a particularly strong cuff from Little Boy, she ducked, prepared for the unexpected. Little Boy, lost in admiration at the terrific power of his blow, was taken off-guard. The bag swung back and knocked him clean off his feet, sending him sprawling in the dirt, rolling over and over before he managed to right himself. Then he dived for the cover of the camphor bush. Before long the two of them worked out that if they launched themselves at the bag and held on, it couldn't swing back vindictively. Instead, they would swing with it.

The cubs were mimicking an attack on prey. When hunting, a leopard will leap at its prey, grapple itself into position with the front paws and force it to the ground by shifting its weight. Then, it will bite at the throat. The game became more complex: the cubs discovered that an unsatisfactory landing could be righted by repositioning the grip of the front paws. With the back legs freed, they could kick like rabbits and disembowel the bag, sending the grass scattering. Or they could anchor the landing, freeing up the front paws.

The cubs needed to bring some finesse to their assault, paying special attention to positioning. Their tails suddenly became useful in balancing. In the leap, adjustment of the tail assisted with the accuracy of their landing. Soon they had the manoeuvre – good energy from the back legs in the jump, unswerving focus with the eyes in case of some eccentric movement, critical placement of the front paws. At the moment of landing, the front paws needed to lift momentarily and then come down decisively to encircle the girth of the bag. Then, claws unsheathed, they needed to grip the soft texture of the hessian. That was it – total possession of the prey.

Soon the hessian bag became a favourite game. We saw it swinging from the tamboti tree, a cub clinging ferociously as it grappled into position for the final and fatal bite.

And so the cubs learned to hold on, which had been Elmon's idea from the beginning. They were on their way to becoming hunters.

# CHAPTER FOUR

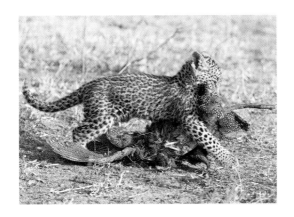

## *Siyaphila*

*We are fine*

Autumn was behind us. These months hold for a shy moment in the lowveld, between the long humid summers and the brief cold winters, as if the subtle character of the season sits uncomfortably with the volatile nature of the African continent.

It was the time of the winter solstice, marking mid-winter in the South. The days were short and crisp. The mists of early morning dispersed slowly, after lingering in wraith-like trails in the lower lying beds of the donga. On early morning walks with the cubs, the sharpness of the icy air bit, burning the delicate lining of the nasal passages and bringing tears to the eyes.

There was a clarity to the light in that early part of the day – pure and crystalline. By evening the dust, kicked up by the many pounding hooves, was held suspended in gusts of wind. As the sun sank, its rays filtered through the thorn bushes, striking the dust-laden air. Refracted, it settled on the landscape a golden patina while distorting the sun into a large scarlet orb.

In the bushveld, the grasses give the winter landscape its particular palette, drying to graded shades of bleached bone colour, creating an Impressionistic look. The trees stand bare, exposing skeletal branches spiked with dry thorns, bringing to the bushveld the beauty of the fallow months.

Energised by the zing in the winter air, Little Boy and Little Girl burst out of their boma for the dawn walks in a frenzy of energy. Noses moist, their fur bushy and raised against the cold, they dashed and zigzagged in a series of arches, leaps and pounces of no particular purpose other than to express the joy of being alive. After expending their initial burst of energy in mock attacks on each other and on our ankles, the cubs would sit dreamily in a shaft of sunlight.

Our afternoon walks were much earlier than in summer because of the shorter days. Often these walks didn't take us as far from the camp, especially when the cubs showed a preference for a round of hide and seek, ambush, or tree-tumbling games in the donga. Sometimes, if the day in the camp had been busy, they would nap during these mellow afternoon sessions and we would rest with them or weave grass bangles, plucking, plaiting and twisting the stems in the way Lawrence and Andries had taught us.

These two brothers were Shangaans from neighbouring Mozambique, two of many refugees who had made their way southwest from the poverty and strife of war. Ignoring geographical boundaries and their illegality as aliens, they became absorbed into the network of rural black people – the families and clans of Shangaan people which extend east across South Africa, northwards into Mozambique. On their exodus, several refugees crossed on foot through the Kruger National Park, a journey fraught with the dangers of confronting wild animals or capture by Park officials and subsequent repatriation. Few of them achieved the refugee's ultimate dream of obtaining a work permit, as Lawrence and Andries had done.

The cubs' confidence in us had grown. Before their midday sleep they played around the camp, experiencing us as we went about tidying around the tents, writing up notes, cleaning film equipment or reading. In a sense the roles were reversed, with the cubs observing us in fascination.

The situation lent itself to hopelessly silly encounters. Little Girl once sneaked under the flap of Karin's tent. She was barely in, when she reversed out hastily, her nose wrinkled and whiskers twitching, rubbing at her face with her paws. Karin was burning incense. Little Girl usually learnt from experience, but she was, after all, a cat. So with a curiosity that was insatiable, it wasn't long before she was back, ferreting around the washstand. She knocked it over, sending the toothbrush, toothpaste, hairbrush and a bar of sandalwood soap scattering to the ground. After the incense episode, we thought the scent of the soap would bother her. But she rubbed her head fondly against the soap, as one who had discovered something essential missing from her life. Her attachment to the smell of soap, eccentric as it was, remained with her. Shortly after this, Little Girl discovered the joys of fabric softener. She would rub against the bottle with a look of bliss on her face and do elaborate shoulder rolls over it.

Little Boy experienced an aspect of human behaviour that flummoxed him and left him with serious doubts about the competence of humans, if the expression on his face was anything to go by. Graham had a rope hanging from a tall spike thorn tree outside his tent and did his fitness exercises there. One afternoon, after much grunting, pulling and stretching, heaving himself up and down the rope for the benefit of his biceps, he noticed Little Boy hiding behind a bush. Little Boy was staring at him quizzically, his pupils completely dilated in alarm but not running away, so riveted was he by Graham's puerile and unsuccessful efforts to climb the tree.

The tents soon became the focus of the cubs' games and the object of their demolition runs. Their claws drawn across the canvas made a screeching sound, which set our nerves on edge. Above all they loved the bouncy effect of launching themselves onto the flysheet. The tautness of the canvas would kick back, catapulting them along its length, and they would have to roll and scramble to right themselves before the headlong slide to the ground. Better still, the pitch of the roof enabled them to hide from one another. Once drawn into ambush, they would leap with paws outstretched at one another and roll in a haphazard jumble into the safe, receiving dip of the canvas. From inside the tent, the effect was heightened by the mysterious noises and the bulging and plunging of the canvas. If one of the cubs was exploring inside, the mock terror created by such a rooftop attack was highly effective, the assailant being unseen and undeclared.

One afternoon I was drinking a cup of tea in the mess tent and writing up notes, when Little Boy launched an attack from above in this way. After a while of muffled thudding and thumping, I glanced up to see him hanging upside down over the edge, trying to stick his head into the small gap between the side of the tent and the flysheet. He was trying to work out how he could manoeuvre his way inside. His target was the trommel* in which we hid his dinner. The expression in his eyes was furtive and his ulterior motives made for pure farce. Tears rolled down my face I laughed so hard.

Then I experienced one of those disassociative moments. My consciousness seemed to zoom to a distance and from that perspective, I took in the incongruence of the scene – me sitting and writing up my notes with a three-month old leopard cub hanging upside down, his tail stuck out at right angles to balance himself and his head wedged awkwardly in the gap of the tent. I paused, struck by the uniqueness of the situation and its absurdity. How transient the moment. How far we had progressed as human beings living alongside leopards, that we could interpret these events as everyday and 'normal'.

The cubs had moments of similar realisation. One afternoon walk, while the cubs were snapping branches in the russet bush willow tree, JV lay down on the sandbank and closed his eyes. His relaxed posture invited the cubs to join him, something they often did when the pace of our walks slowed down. Little Girl moved tentatively onto his chest, curled up and promptly fell asleep, lulled by his gentle snoring.

After some moments she awoke and was so alarmed that she hissed and ran up a tree. We both, human and leopard, had created an extra

* trommel: Afrikaans word meaning 'tin trunk'

dimension. For parts of each day we were purely human and they were purely leopard, and then for stretches of that same day, we could relate to one another so freely, it was as if we were of the same species.

Little Boy and Little Girl's play manoeuvres included the early versions of hunting strategies: the pounce, accompanied by the wriggling bottom, the swat and the scoop, which they used when trying to revive dead insects. Play and predation are graded aspects of the same behaviour. Though the cubs were technically too young to hunt, we were eager to create an association in their minds. How were we to set up a hunt?

An ideal opportunity presented itself. To the west of T'Ingwe camp, there are three waterholes which make up Tortoise Pan, situated at the edge of scented thorn woodland. Tall ebonies fringe the pans, drawing their strength from the permanent water that flows through the seep line. In the dry winter months, the surface water of the pan recedes, leaving behind muddy pools. Often, catfish are trapped in this mud, burrowing down deep to wait out the dry season. Initially, the fish become very agitated before making their last bid for survival by burying themselves in the sludge, or as some astonishing stories tell, travelling over land in search of refuge in other water.

There were a number of catfish in Tortoise Pan, wriggling and flapping together in their misery of mud. Little Boy and Little Girl were three months old and our adventures with them were becoming bolder and our range further from T'Ingwe camp. We led them to the pools. The vastness of the landscape, the huge ebonies, the fallen logs at the edge of the water and the long, tangled grass and gwarrie bush dwarfed them.

Both stood for a moment in that attentive way of theirs, with their legs half-bent in a crouch. Then Little Boy swooped in, hardly pausing a beat to assess his environment before launching himself. Whether he recognised the fish as food at first or whether the wriggling movement attracted him, I don't know. He began his attack with two or three charges at the fish, swerving at the final moment and backing off. The fish were too big for him to cope with, but leopards have an astonishing ability to handle large prey by utilising their extraordinary power, suppleness and manoeuvrability. On his third run at the fish, Little Boy pounced on its back, landing on all fours, his body smaller than the length of the fish. He clung on to the writhing fish and laid his teeth into its back, gripping it and shaking it vigorously. The fish naturally flapped all the more. This startled Little Boy for a brief moment, but he was not deterred from the prospect of a good hunt. His ears swivelling with effort, he dragged the fish under the gwarrie bush next to the pan, growling ferociously in a way we had never heard from him before. The bush obscured his killing technique. It appeared that he had finished off the fish by biting it repeatedly. His fierce determination made up for his lack of mastery. Little Boy had executed his first hunt.

Little Girl, meanwhile, headed straight for the cover of the tangled grass and raisin bush. She peeped out to survey the area, identifying all avenues of escape and potential threats in the sounds and smells of the place before she allowed herself to entertain any thoughts of eating.

The area around the pan is fairly open, but there is a section of low-lying shrubbery and fallen logs. We hoped that the cubs might identify these as cover and work their way towards the fish before setting up their stalk-and-pounce. From under the bush, Little Girl squinted at her brother, quite piqued that he had found food. From the look in her eyes, she was hoping to pirate a piece. Little Boy, fiercely defensive of his prey, growled at her in such a way that I feared he would hurt her. The dominance he expressed over meat seemed more exaggerated than ever.

We tried to help Little Girl in her own hunt by indicating the way to the pan via the cover and making scooping movements into the water with our hands for her to imitate. I'm not sure whether that helped or confused her. Finally, she found enough courage to edge towards the remaining fish in the pool by way of a branch that hung over the water and then batted and scooped at them from above. She lacked the conviction she needed for the carry-through. We were distressed by her timidity and, not wanting to see her confidence eroded, we scooped a fish out of the water. We gave it to her live. She grabbed it in her mouth with a firm and resolute bite and looked upwards and around her for a tree in which to hoist it. Not finding anything that satisfied her, she retreated to the cover of the gwarrie bush where she had hidden before, and there she too repeatedly bit the fish. When she was satisfied that it was dead, she began to eat it.

The different hunting strategies of the two young cubs parallelled their individual characters. Little Girl was still circumspect as she stood straddling the dead fish, her eyes darting here and there and her ears swivelling, alert to any sound of possible danger. Little Boy showed no caution at all. Attacking his fish with such energy and mock-killing it with ferocious growls, he ate it in a noisy and obvious way. Little Boy had been reckless. Any passing hyenas would have been alerted and stolen the kill from him, injuring him or even killing him in the process had he been foolish enough to try to defend it.

The hunting experiment encouraged us to give the cubs whole carcasses of the creatures they encountered on their walks – birds and small game, such as hares. We hoped to create a strong incentive to practise hunting by association – that which they saw live and around them was what they needed to catch. When we gave the cubs a carcass, they hunted it relentlessly, stalking from a short distance and pouncing on it, batting it into the air, scooping it up from the ground with an upward curved movement of the paws as it fell, encouraging the dead creature to make a last effort to escape, so they could go through the exciting motions of the kill all over again. And while the cubs played, they learned where to hold the carcass and how to bite it.

In the early winter months, an elderly Shangaan named Jackson, who lived in the local village, came to help us in the camp. He'd been in the conservancy his entire life, living at first in a traditional hunter-gatherer community, before game reserves were officially declared in the area and the subsistence hunting by the local people outlawed. The only hunting that continued thereafter was that on the privately owned land adjacent to what became the Kruger National Park. Jackson, as a young man, had hired his services to hunting parties that visited the area in the 1950s and 60s.

When eco-tourism and photographic safaris spread to the private reserves, hunting came to an end. Jackson adapted his bush skills as a hunter to become a tracker, locating the game for tourists. Now in his retirement, he lived in the neighbouring Shangaan area. Because of his long-held association with the Varty family, we found work for him in our camp when he came looking to supplement his pension.

His job was to build our evening campfire, to light the paraffin lamps and position them around the camp, to fill the water cart and to clean the cubs' boma. Jackson moved about the camp with a slow and shuffling gait, keeping very much to himself and seldom saying much. Sadly, his natural reticence kept him from sharing with us what must have been a wealth of stories from the hunting era. He had the face that artists love to sketch, etched with lines of wisdom and experience. He communicated much through the expressions revealed there.

Little Boy and Little Girl stalked Jackson around the camp relentlessly. Perhaps it was because he was slight in build and stooped with age, or perhaps it was the predictability of his activities around the camp. Most likely it was his prone posture as he bent over the paraffin lamps, trimming the wick and topping up the fuel, or again as he bent over the water cart while filling it, or over the logs while lighting the fire, blowing at the small flame of the kindling.

It wasn't as if old Jackson was unaware of these hidden assailants. Often I would see a small, slightly suppressed smile hidden in the lines of his face and in his eyes, clouded blue with the cataracts of advancing age. The irony of his life, first as a hunter, and now as a servant to the same creatures he had spent a lifetime with in violent confrontation, was not lost on him. In all the time he tended our camp, the cubs never once pounced or even scratched him, but they stalked him relentlessly, excited out of their wits by the sheer possibility. I suspect that, despite the impression he made of being easy prey, his lifetime of living with wild creatures had sharpened the instincts that kept him half a beat ahead of them.

We kept visitors to T'Ingwe camp to a minimum, and those who came drew an intriguing reaction from Little Boy and Little Girl. The cubs would conceal themselves, their body posture indicating their alertness and readiness to bolt, and then stare penetratingly at the visitor for a long time. On the level of instinct, their response following the initial going-over was fairly easy to predict. A small child with jerky movements and a high-pitched voice, or anyone with a shuffling gait or a limp, activated their predatory instincts. Young, injured or infirm prey would automatically select itself as being the easiest to hunt.

Significantly, too, anyone who was nervous or hesitant in the presence of the cubs was targeted immediately. Little Boy and Little Girl would challenge their victims maliciously, with transparent delight in the fear they inspired. When those who understood this cat language called their bluff with a direct counter-challenge, the cubs would turn tail in fright and bolt.

Their treatment of visitors revealed intriguing cooperation. In collusion, they worked out a tactic of intimidation. Little Boy would approach a visitor directly with his head slightly lowered, mild aggression in his eyes mixed with curiosity. Little Girl would move in a half-circle at the edge of things, hiding behind the water cart, slipping through the shadows cast by the mess tent, behind the canvas flap and from there, assess the situation. This strategic manoeuvre, indicating cooperation, is not typically seen between two leopards. At the point where the half-circle of

Little Girl's path of approach intersected with Little Boy's direct line, they would join forces, standing together and staring with hostility at the visitor, bodies lowered in a half-crouch, as if ready to leap. The effect of this combined confrontation of two leopards moving towards them simultaneously, but from different angles, unnerved even the bravest of strangers.

Visitors to the camp were well-briefed never to turn their backs on the cubs, to crouch or to run off, should they be challenged. Predators interpret these movements as an opportunity to attack. I suspect that for people unfamiliar with wild animals, the briefing created a tension and an atmosphere of anticipation, which was tangible to the cubs. They responded with increased excitement. The tension worked in their favour, as a feedback loop, exaggerating the threat of attack. The two of them worked the situation like professionals. The cubs were not lethal, but from our own experience, we were aware of the power and the phenomenal speed in those tiny bodies. Although their claws and their teeth were still small, should they have really wished to cause harm, I suspect they could have.

I was curious about the way the cubs stared at visitors. At first, I thought it was because their visual acuity was not completely developed, but I came to think that perhaps they were 'scanning' the person. Rather than merely taking in a one-dimensional visual picture, they were making a more global assessment, a composite picture of body posture, the nature of the stranger's movement, the sound they made, the quality of their personal energy field.

This way of looking was related to survival, yet it called to mind the way Mother Leopard looked at me. Hers was a gaze that appeared to see beyond the mundane. I always felt she was seeing beyond my outward form, to a more essential part, as if the physical concerns of what she needed to know had been taken care of by her senses in an automatic way, freeing up her mind. Initially, I had interpreted this as hostility, so cool and detached was the feeling accompanying it. Gradually, I began to feel a sense of lightness, of being released from the obligatory human pretences and defences, leaving me with a sense of her knowing me rather than seeing me.

I wasn't alone in this feeling – I know that others who met her commented on the experience, saying it was as if she was looking right through them.

Other visitors to the camp were of the furry or feathered variety. They were both curious and opportunistic. Initially, our camp was a sphere of human isolation, as the inhabitants of the bush held back in an invisible circle, cautious of the smell and the sound of us. It was curious being aware of unseen eyes watching us from all around, and hearing the news of our presence broadcast along the bush telegraph.

Cheeky troops of vervet monkeys were the first to investigate us more closely, spying from the acacia trees, bobbing up and down and chattering unhappily amongst themselves. The presence of a predator always has them in a state of high excitement and fear, clambering for the top of the trees to sound their indignant alarm. All the other residents of the bush link to this intricate warning network, which covers a wide radius and tells of the goings-on. The monkeys at T'Ingwe camp were confused by Little Boy and Little Girl, always expecting the cubs' mother to be around the next corner.

Hyenas are usually the first visitors to venture right into a bush camp, with their extraordinary sense of smell and opportunism. They were soon scavenging from our rubbish bins. Early mornings found us gathering rubbish strewn far and wide around the camp. We were concerned that they would eat large chunks of the rubber bin itself, which might do them a serious injury, so we strung the bin high up in a tree out of their reach and lowered it up and down on a pulley. It was good though for the cubs to see and smell hyenas from the safety of their boma. In the early months, hyenas are one of the most dangerous threats to a young leopard cub, and they remain lifelong adversaries.

Gradually, all manner of insects and rodents signalled their acceptance of our presence by moving into the camp. There was a gerbil – a small mouse-like rodent – that moved into the mess tent, making its burrow in the ground under the plastic floor sheeting. The cubs played endless games with the creature, but to their frustration, it always remained concealed and beyond their reach. The scratching noises drove the cubs to distraction. The occasional moving lump under the floor sheet worked them into a frenzy as they leapt and pounced and slid around the mess tent in an ongoing attempt to catch him.

It wasn't the cubs that put an end to the gerbil's life. Sadly, one morning we found him drowned in their water bowl. Little Girl scooped his body out and batted him around eagerly. But there were no signs of life, leaving both cubs gazing at the wet and bedraggled corpse in bafflement.

On our morning and evening walks, we now were moving within about a 100-metre radius from the camp. Little Boy and Little Girl began to identify set stopping points, which were landmarks or beacons of some kind. Little Girl was always particular about visiting the trees. In some discreet way, which I could never see but rather sense, she had a polite exchange of greeting with them.

We were directing the cubs towards a territorial patrol – when leopards acquaint themselves with events in their home range. The cubs showed their familiarity with the area through repetitive behaviour and through exploring any changes in the 'territory' they had loosely defined for themselves. They chose the same paths to walk, sniffed at the same bushes and used the same trees for tree-tumbling games and for reconnoitre. They used vantage points such as the termite mounds or rocks. Little Girl especially, was particular about this practice.

In a more mature leopard, this patrol behaviour develops into a set procedure. Selected trees become scratching posts, where deposits of scent from glands between the leopard's claws tell of its passing. Certain bushes will be used for urine spraying, to state its presence in the area. In this way, a leopard will analyse the complexity of events in its territory and from the information left behind by other leopards, identify any potential threats.

Tree-climbing became an obsession with Little Girl. Her brother was content to bounce around, hurling himself at unlikely branches, clutching on with his front paws as he tumbled like a bear cub, with his bottom swinging and his tail flicking as he tried to right himself. Little Girl leapt lightly, landing delicately with the precision of one who is born to the task. Often she would look at her brother as he bounded around with a look of censure at his disregard for the higher nature of the trees, which she clearly respected. There were distinct moments when, after climbing into its branches, she would stand motionless, as if in communion with the tree, connecting with the energy flowing from it.

There was still much to be learned from the trees. The various kinds of bark had different properties that could either assist their claws and give them traction for climbing, or else resist them. These textures affected the speed and certainty with which they could scale trees. Little Boy and Little Girl needed to identify which trees were useful, which provided a good branch structure for a larder. Often a scavenging hyena would be after them, attempting to pirate their prey.

When the cubs were about four months old, they came across zebra dung for the first time. Dung conveys a wealth of information. The cubs sniffed at it, rolled on it and urinated on it, delighted by their find and responding vigorously to whatever story it carried. Then they began testing it to extract the secrets of its origins. They were not eating the dung, but by rolling bits between their teeth they could absorb the chemical odour molecules through the vomeronasal organ in the nasal passages connected to the mouth. From there, its message would pass to their brain and be stored for future reference.

Wild cats often roll bodily in the dung of other animals, apparently enjoying the smell and, as some observers say, disguising their own predator scent under the scent of the prey-species. This theory, if true, elevates the ability of the big cats to strategise a hunt, in this case by deception, to the level of genius.

Deep into the dry season of the winter months, we came across fresh elephant tracks, not far from T'Ingwe camp. We thought these belonged to the bull elephants that habitually traversed the riverine bush and donga system, seeking out the green and succulent vegetation. After sniffing at the tracks with curiosity, Little Boy ran up a tree and meowed plaintively. Up ahead were indeed two bull companions tussling playfully, testing their strength against one another by locking tusks and shoving with all their might.

This is one of nature's endearing tableaux. It is such a mixture of comedy and earnestness. Amiable pairs of young bulls, evicted from the cowherd for being too precocious, will tag along with one another, facing adventures together. Sometimes linking up with an older bull for guidance, they wander in and out of adolescent trouble until maturity, when they can establish themselves as breeding bulls with more serious social responsibilities.

Both Little Girl and Little Boy were terrified by the sheer size of the creatures and the piercing sound of their trumpeting. Even when the bulls quietened down, the cubs, hiding in the tree, shifted their bodies uncomfortably on the branches, as if responding to some invisible cue. Were they sensing the infrasonic rumble that elephants use to communicate, as it travelled through the earth and vibrated up the tree trunks?

When the bulls trumpeted in exuberance, the intensity of the sound was such a shock to Little Boy that he fell out of the tree, rolled over and then scrambled off as fast as his legs could carry him. We were crouched behind a clump of gwarrie bush, not intervening so that the cubs would make what they could of this new experience. Little Girl was well hidden in the tree, welded to the branch in fear, her entire body taut as steel. An involuntary, high-pitched meow alerted one of the elephants and he looked up, directly meeting Little Girl's gaze.

Despite the huge mass, rolling bulk and powerful presence surrounding elephants, there is paradoxically an aura of immense stillness about them. The older bull companion looked up steadily at Little Girl in a long, considered pause and then made a cursory statement of authority by blasting air vigorously down the length of his trunk at the sand on the donga floor. Finding himself that close to a human or a larger predator, he almost certainly would have mock-charged. Perhaps, suspecting that the cubs were alone while their mother was away hunting, he'd held back his full aggression, making only a token gesture to teach them a lesson. Taking as much time as he felt appropriate, he sauntered off.

Inevitably on our walks, we came across a host of insects, birds and lizards. Little Boy stalked a chagra one day with an expertise that amazed us. He came closer to catching it than he had to catching anything since the Great Fish Hunt at Tortoise Pan. Even though the bird shrieked and escaped his pounce, Little Boy was delighted with his work and surprised at missing it.

Francolins, game birds similar to small grouse, were a constant source of frustration and irritation. They fly only if they have to, preferring to scratch around in the dirt for insects amongst the shrubs and grasses. As we walked they would fly up out of the grass, shrieking raucously, start-ling all of us. Gradually, the francolin population of the area began to tease the cubs by parading and strutting back and forth ahead of us, prompting the cubs into an automatic crouch with their bottoms wiggling in the air. Then, as the cubs pounced, they fluttered off elusively into a tree, crowing victory.

With time, Little Girl came to ignore them, glancing disdainfully in the opposite direction when they began their teasing. Little Boy fell for their trickery every time, believing that if he applied more power and strength, he might one day succeed. He never did manage to catch a francolin because he was too impatient. Yet Nature works in ingenious ways, and between the taunting of the francolin and his fierce determination, Little Boy refined his hunting tactics.

Walking with the cubs gave us insight into the way they experienced their environment. They lived in a world of sensory information, and everything they did indicated their super-sensitivity to the stimuli around them. When Little Girl showed overdue interest in a branch lying across the path, I initially thought, by the tension that showed in her body, that she had mistaken it for a snake. I couldn't work out why it took so long for her to discover her error. She skirted the branch, looked at it askance and then sniffed at it nervously, drawing her head back sharply as if it were some living thing.

It had been torn from a tree by a passing elephant, whose scent must have lingered on it. For Little Girl, the experience was different. It was not the branch alone that she was responding to, but the bigger picture. She was recreating the mysterious events that related to a piece of a tree, a life form which she understood better than most, lying broken on the path and smelling like an elephant.

Getting the cubs back to the camp at night was becoming difficult. Little Girl insisted on sitting high up in a tree as dusk fell. With their increasing size and strength, they were not easy to handle. Previously, if they had shown reluctance, we would scoop them up and carry them. I understood why Little Girl resisted coming back to the boma in the evening. Dusk is an invigorating time for most predators, but especially for leopards, whose powers rise with the darkness and whose energies resonate with that of the moon. Just as things were becoming interesting with the birds chanting their evening song, the air cooling, the angle of the light changing and the shadows lengthening – all the cues which prompted her instinctively to become more alert to what the night promised, we would head back to camp.

We had programmed the cubs with classical Pavlovian conditioning to circumvent this problem. Right from when the cubs were little, we whistled when we gave them meat, creating an association of food with the sound of the whistle. When we found the cubs were beginning to show more interest in tree climbing than coming home, we whistled. Little Boy flew haphazardly down the tree without a thought. At first Little Girl responded, taking a more dignified route down the tree. Eventually, she saw through the trickery and ignored it with the contempt it deserved.

The pattern continued, as the cubs grew older, Little Boy remaining easier to bring home than his sister because of his passion for food. After we discarded the whistle, we clattered the enamel plate. His ears would prick up regardless of what he was doing and he'd bolt back to the camp. Food had a place in Little Girl's life but when she was deep into exploring, or in that meditative mode she'd adopt when communing with trees, we found it almost impossible to get her to return. While her brother was winding his body and tail eagerly around our legs, to remind us that we were best friends, high-stepping around the tent while making intense food noises, Little Girl would remain sitting peacefully in her tree, her attention directed elsewhere in the ether.

At times like this, we took it in turns to sit with her until she finally moved. She would have been easy prey to the hyenas that roved the area had she come down from her tree at the wrong moment. Graham held the record for patience, once sitting under a tree for six hours with Little Girl in the higher reaches.

Little Girl hated to be separated from her beloved brother, so we used poor Little Boy as a lure. We held him as he squirmed, howled and tried to wrestle free, while walking up and down under Little Girl's tree. When she had seen Little Boy leaving without her, we would race back to camp and inevitably she would follow soon after.

It was curious that Little Girl was so attached to her brother, for in leopard culture, detachment is key. In all other ways she responded to the way of leopards. For example, if she heard the threatening barks of baboons, she would abandon her food to run for safety. Little Boy acknowledged the presence of danger by eating faster with his eyes glowing and then making off, reluctantly, with as much food in his mouth as he could carry, his cheeks bulging. For Little Boy, food was the most important reason for living, except perhaps for his delight in bouncing off the branches of the russet bush willow tree.

Big cats can consume up to 10 per cent of their body weight in one meal, tending to gorge on a kill and then eat nothing for a few days. A full-grown female leopard at about 35 kilograms and a male at 55 kilograms, need to hunt once or twice a week, depending on the size of the prey. Preferred prey at Londolozi is impala, duiker, bushbuck and small antelope. Warthog is also a good catch, giving them more than 30 kilograms of meat. If it is safely stashed in the branches of a tree, it can keep them for nearly a week.

Little Boy's gorging instinct was in keeping with wild leopard behaviour, except that he liked to feast all the time, without the periods of fast. He threw out our weighing charts chronically. One week we were astounded to find how much weight he had gained over and above the usual half a kilogram both cubs were gaining weekly. We discovered later that he had successfully raided both his and Little Girl's food supply for that day, just hours before the weighing session. Little Boy could never resist the offer of a snack and traded favours in exchange for food bribes.

Little Girl's eating needs reflected her state of mind. If she was tense or nervous she would lose her appetite, but if she was balanced she would eat well. She never gulped no matter how hungry she was, always displaying delicacy and grace. The finesse Little Girl brought to the activity of eating, the precision and economy, was an art form. The first whole mammal Little Girl tackled was a scrub hare. She plucked away at the fur, spitting it out carefully, clearing a neat patch of skin on the hindquarters and licking the remaining strands with her tongue. Then, meticulous as a surgeon, she bit with her incisors to penetrate the skin. Finally, she turned her head sideways to get at the flesh with her carnassials. Methodically she ate her fill, working her way from the rear of the carcass to the less accessible meat, before finally licking off any bits remaining on the larger bones.

Once the cubs realised that food originated from the mess tent, they spent patient hours trying to track it down. After establishing that the meat was kept in the metal cupboard in the kitchen, their attempts to steal it, especially Little Boy's, grew more determined and ingenious. This had less to do with hunger, in Little Girl's case, than the determination to succeed.

Little Boy's modus operandi was to sneak behind the cupboard and then run at it, throwing his full weight at it with a heavy thump. Little Girl knew the secret had something to do with the door handles, and would rise up on her back legs and bat at them hopefully.

Defeated, they changed their angle of entry and approached it from above, angling into the mess tent between the gap of the flysheet and the side wall. They found themselves – to their great frustration – on top of the cupboard, not having achieved their goal.

Little Girl's diligence about her grooming rituals showed the same meticulous precision that she brought to the art of eating. Grooming is so much more than washing for a cat – each time the roughly barbed tongue runs across the fur, sebaceous glands attached to the roots are stimulated, releasing secretions that keep the fur water-resistant. The saliva cools the body through evaporation.

When grooming, the cubs followed a typical pattern, applying saliva to the inside of the paw and then running it upwards over their faces, repeating the action over and over in circular motions and then working behind the ear. A switch of paw across to the other side and then, the top half done, long strokes to the front legs, flanks and the anal-genital region, to remove bits of thorn and grit, loose hair and skin parasites. Perhaps it was the early flicker of maternal instincts that urged her to take care of him, for occasionally Little Girl tried her ministrations on her brother. I seldom saw him reciprocating. Manicuring was a precise and meticulous business. She would flex and extend her claws, working methodically on each one with her teeth until satisfied that all the dirt had been removed. Afterwards, she stretched her paw in front of her face to examine it from a slight distance, assessing her work with a calm and critical gaze.

All cats have a natural sensuality. While grooming, Little Boy stretched luxuriously, arching his back, extending his tail and curving his paws around his face. Yet the business-like expression in his eyes indicated that his underlying attitude was more utilitarian. He was less meticulous than Little Girl, but applied himself with more vigour, as if he wished to be done with it and get on with more entertaining things. Little Girl indulged extravagantly in the sensuous pleasures of her ablutions, the look in her eyes one of sheer bliss.

It came sooner than we expected. One July morning, the cubs were very reluctant to come out of their boma. When they did, they crouched low to the ground, repeatedly sniffing at patches of dirt as they edged nervously towards the donga. Clearly something was echoing in their minds – some unformed knowledge, circling close to awareness but not quite in their experience.

We heard an elephant in the vicinity, the sharp snap of branches cutting through the stillness of the morning. Deep rumbles of communication followed. At first we thought that might be what was disturbing the cubs, but their repeated sniffing soon persuaded us that it was a particular scent left in the area by another animal that was causing the trouble.

Another leopard had moved into the area, investigating the telltale scent of Little Boy and Little Girl. Initially there were no tracks, but scent markings lay close to the camp.

Olfactory signalling is a sophisticated form of communication between leopards. Their scent-marking equipment includes secretions of the anal glands, emptied when they urinate on scent posts, and released by interdigital glands on the paws when they scratch. The range of chemicals in the secretions produces a vocabulary of signals about the individual's age, rank or status, sexual receptivity and even mood. In leopard society, the message is a discreet distance signal, intended to inform and so to avoid unexpected physical confrontation. This is vital in leopard social dynamics to reduce the risk of injury from a fight. To a solitary hunter, this could mean dying of starvation while being unable to hunt. If aggression is inevitable between leopards, for example in the defence of cubs or territory, it is intentional and seldom through accidental encounter.

The scent messages the cubs were detecting that morning were possibly those of another female, looking to claim territory. She would in all likelihood be a young animal, tentative and without the conviction of a mature female defending an established home range. She might harass the cubs, even injure them, but she would be cautious, confused about the absence of their mother. If it were the resident male that had left his calling card, the threat to the cubs was grave. He would be ruthless. He hadn't fathered them and they were a challenge to his genetic tenure.

We were all upset. Elmon searched everywhere for tracks, but even with his skills, he could find no definite evidence to tell us whether it was a male or a female. We were almost certain that the secretive nature of this visitor in the night indicated that it was an adult leopard. If it had been a lion or hyena, we would have certainly found tracks, as their behavioural style is one of boldness.

The mood around our camp that morning was glum. Although there were other dangers in the world we shared with our cubs – the possibility of suddenly coming across lion or elephant on our walks, or of hyenas sneaking into camp when we were at our least vigilant – the threat of a leopard was more sinister. It is such a ruthless and elusive animal to have as an opponent. We collected some fresh elephant dung and gave it to the cubs to play with to distract them from their troubles. Elephant dung was their favourite. Before long, the balls of dung did their work. The cubs cheered up as they shoulder-rolled over it, passed small bits between their teeth, urinated on it, sniffed it, lay on it and knocked it around, batting clumps of it with great joy between their front paws.

Was it coincidental? Shortly after we became aware of the presence of the wild leopard, the cubs started a new elimination ritual. Up until then, the cubs had used the inside of their boma for urinating and defecating, regardless of the proximity of their sleeping place or water bowl. Oddly enough, the water bowl was more than once the target. Now the cubs waited for their walks and, once outside their boma, would eliminate in a carefully chosen spot.

They were too young to scent-mark by spraying urine. Marking in this way is a significant rite of passage in a leopard's growth to maturity. Territory is proclaimed, sexual readiness advertised and other business of adulthood communicated. Until the arrival of the wild leopard, both cubs had shown preliminary marking behaviour, random kicking and scratching in the sand in response to a scent cue left on a bush by other animals, but no actual spraying. It was as if Little Boy and Little Girl were responding to the foreign leopard's message with their own calling card saying 'We are here too!'

We continued urging the cubs to hunt, trying to impart a sense of purpose in the way we spoke on our walks and with our body talk, crouching down low and moving forward cautiously. We paid close attention to what lay ahead, hoping that the cubs would catch on that we were striding purposefully in the way of all predators, in search of prey. More often than not, when we did come across a game bird or a scrub hare, the cubs would give themselves away by choosing an inappropriate ambush place, or flick their tails so that the white tip waved in the air like a flag. Sometimes, their stalking was just too obvious.

In the wild, leopard cubs are catching small prey by the age of about seven months. Up until that point, anything that they manage to secure for themselves by way of insects or grasshoppers is sheer luck. The cubs were only four months old.

There was a young male cub at Londolozi, whose mother had dispersed him to independence at the early age of eight months. He survived his sub-adulthood by hanging around a dam for months on end, hunting frogs. The game scouts from the lodge monitored his progress closely, but no one ever saw him eating anything else or found evidence of skin or bones to suggest that he'd caught other prey. While that is the exception, it does show how adaptable leopards can be.

The impulse to pounce at anything that moves is overwhelmingly strong in young cubs. Encouraged by their hunting fluke in the Great Fish Hunt, Little Boy and Little Girl were relentless, flying at anything that fluttered, scurried, flapped or buzzed.

Little Boy accidentally caught a grasshopper after one of these frenzied dashes. As it wiggled in his mouth, confusion passed over his face, closely followed by a look of distaste. Many grasshoppers release a nasty-tasting and sometimes poisonous fluid when captured. Little Boy held the grasshopper loosely in his mouth, his eyes cast downwards, as he struggled inwardly with the realisation that his prey was inedible. Finally, he spat it out and loped off good-naturedly. Little Boy was always optimistic. Next time would be better. Besides, he was now a hunter.

We anticipated that it might be Little Girl who would one day make the first 'real' kill. When we came across a small herd of impala in a clearing to the south of the donga one morning, she heard their movements long before any of us did, although we had almost walked right up to them. She fell into a crouch, followed by an impressive stalk up the slope of the bank. Although the impala scattered, her instincts were right on track, both in the way she had set about her hunt and in her readiness to make the most of an opportunity.

Little Girl's mind stayed in hunting mode. Further down the clearing, she found a warthog burrow in a termite mound. She slipped down the entrance, no doubt attracted by the smell of the prey. She was lucky no one was at home, as warthog have a habit of charging out of their burrows at full steam if they fear that a predator is about to dig them out. Despite being short in the legs, they carry a sturdy body and are tough-minded. They defend themselves and their young with the most courageous counter-attack. Their boldness can surprise even an experienced predator. They have formidable recurved tusks, which slice viciously as they charge headlong at their aggressor, often inflicting lethal wounds.

We watched Little Boy and Little Girl keenly to see whether there was any instinctive fear in going down the warthog burrow. Was this one of the lessons they would have learnt from their mother? Clearly, Little Girl had no idea or sense of danger even though, by the fresh tracks at the entrance, the burrow was in current use and she must surely have scented the recent presence of the hog.

I wondered how a mother leopard would have handled this. We banged on the ground and shouted. Little Girl ignored us completely. She was obviously so enjoying the snugness of her hidyhole. I tried to convey a sense of danger in my mood, tone of voice and body posture and even tried sending mental messages of dangerous warthogs. My efforts were in vain, judging by the animated expressions on Little Boy's face. This was another adventure and the cubs were oblivious to danger.

The adrenalin rush following the attempted impala hunt of the morning hadn't subsided. That same afternoon, Little Girl launched herself after a duiker we chanced upon in the thicket. Little Boy loped along good-naturedly with her, but without the same intensity of purpose. The chase was long and was more about fun than about results. A leopard, once it has missed its prey with its first pounce, is unlikely to run it down over any kind of distance. This chase involved determined jogging and crashing through the bush to keep up with the cubs. The noise we created would have frightened any prey within kilometres, but we were afraid the cubs would be carried away by the momentum of their hunt and get lost.

The cubs' first successful hunt after the Great Fish Hunt became known as 'the Battle with the Leguvaan'. It happened on the branches of the favourite russet bush willow tree, which provided a perfect spot for the ambush. The leguvaan was lying on a branch when the cubs spotted it. Hardly pausing to stalk, they fell into a preliminary crouch, wriggling their bottoms. Then, with their leading paws raised and slightly curved, they pounced.

A leguvaan looks like an overgrown lizard. Under attack, its defence is to sham dead, a tactic it uses with rare perfection. If captured, it will suffer itself to be beaten, bitten and rolled around, accepting blow after blow, hoping that its assailant, having exhausted the pleasures of the hunt, will pause, put off by the passivity of its prey, and then lose interest. Then, when the way is clear, the leguvaan miraculously comes alive and makes its escape.

This leguvaan lay quite still while Little Boy and Little Girl threw him repeatedly into the air, to land on the ground with a dull thud. They flicked him this way and that, rolled over their shoulders onto him, smacking, biting and taking it in turns to stalk and pounce and 'kill' the creature over and over again.

Another type of leguvaan defence is a painful bite. It latches onto its attacker with its tiny but razor-sharp teeth, hoping by its tenacity to unnerve its assailant. Sure enough, after a few rounds of battery, the leguvaan lashed out and bit Little Boy on his foot, holding on tightly. Little Boy leapt around, trying in vain to throw it off. He bucked and writhed, thrashing this way and that with his tail, with the leguvaan firmly attached to his paw. Eventually, the leguvaan let go and Little Boy retreated, crestfallen, limping pitifully with his eyes downcast and his ears angled sideways. He gazed mournfully at us in his defeat. A canine lost in the fight gave his face a comical lop-sided look as he opened his mouth, gasping for breath.

The cubs were emerging into early adulthood, losing their woolly fur, at first on the upper parts of their forelegs. This fluffy, raised fur gave way to a sleeker variety, creating a distinct line between the old coat and the new, which lay flat against their bodies. Little Boy's new coat emerged on his legs almost overnight, making him look like a pom-pom with legs.

Then, for no apparent reason, his second canine simply disappeared. Was he lacking some minerals in his diet, despite our meticulous efforts?

Leopards lose their primary teeth. Often their permanent teeth emerge while the first are still in place, giving them four upper canines for a brief period, before the adult teeth push away the other teeth. With Little Boy, this didn't happen. With his missing teeth and his odd arrangement of fur, he looked so funny and I was glad it was Little Boy and not Little Girl that we were laughing at. He didn't seem to mind. Actually, he revelled in his newfound attention, even though he was not fully aware of the cause of it. Had it been Little Girl, I think her self-esteem might have suffered and there would have been little chance of persuading my male colleagues to be mindful of her sensitive nature. They would have dismissed my concerns as projected maternalism.

Little Boy's role as the clown of T'Ingwe camp took on a new dimension after his mishap with a candle. We noticed him sniffing gingerly at the candle flame one evening as we sat at the campfire, but we were confident that its heat would soon drive his sensitive nose away. The flame didn't seem to bother him. Soon there was the unmistakable scent of burning fur wafting through the air. We chased him off, but the damage was done.

One entire section of the whiskers over his eye had burnt off completely, leaving the remaining stubble of white whisker in curly frizzles. While this proved the theory that cats have a superior endorphin system to ours, protecting them from pain more effectively, we were concerned about Little Boy's misadventure for another reason. With both canines missing, his coat patchy, his eyebrow sizzled, he was no longer his former handsome self. He looked distinctly silly and his feature film debut was coming up in a couple of weeks.

Little Girl's physical transition from cubhood was more gracious. Her fluff fell away more subtly down her shoulders and legs, revealing a glimpse of her future sleek coat, gleaming amber and russet with ebony rosettes. She suddenly shot up in height but was still tiny in build. She reminded me of a china doll – vulnerable and delicate. Her depth and complexity was reflected in the look of awareness that was almost always in her eyes. By nature she was shy and highly-strung. Curiously, it was she who was becoming the more affectionate of the two cubs.

A fallen leadwood tree lay where Inyatini leads into the main Mashabene Donga, a few hundred metres south of T'Ingwe camp. The cubs enjoyed the visibility up and down the river bed. We spent many, slow hours lying there, absorbing the sociable twittering of birds in the trees, the rustle of the leaves and the ongoing rhythm and music, sharing with the cubs the way they experienced the bush. How full and complex a seemingly quiet afternoon in the bush can be. At times like these, it was Little Girl who would tentatively approach one of us and lie close-by, just touching. It was always such a gift when she did this, such a reaching out from one so timid.

In the cubs' relationship, Little Girl showed more overt affection. Little Boy once vomited seven times in two hours. Leopards do have the ability to induce vomiting voluntarily, to release sharp bone fragments or unacceptable food from their digestive system. We all panicked, thinking that he must be seriously ill, he seemed to be taking so much strain. Little Girl, usually so dependent on her brother's lead, comforted him tenderly. She seemed to know exactly what to do, although she was clearly upset by his distress. She moved in close to him, offering her body for warmth. Little Boy responded meekly by cuddling up to her. He must have been in a state of shock and losing body heat fast, for he allowed himself to be licked and attended to. Finally Little Girl settled down next to him, with Little Boy tucked in close beside her. Somehow, the anxiety on her face had vanished and in its place was an expression of calm attentiveness that reminded me, in human terms, of the coping strength women often find when a loved one needs comfort.

Trying to tap into Little Boy and Little Girl's non-verbal communication became easier as we got to know their individual characters. Of all the mammals, cats have the most complex array of facial gestures and a rich repertoire of body postures, giving them a mute but eloquent communication. Although their voices are expressive, revealing subtler shades of meaning and emphasis, in leopards, vocalisation deals mostly with the more mundane issues, such as calling for a mate, indicating position or demonstrating aggression. It is in the silences, in the spaces between that which is overt, that the complexity of a cat's communication travels.

The extent to which an animal is successful in its life is closely related to its skill in communication. Little Boy and Little Girl had spent such a brief time with their mother, learning the language of leopards, before coming into our care. How were they to continue to learn? In humans, there is a critical period during which language, if not learnt, is lost forever. I was troubled as to how the cubs would fare, as there was little that we could do to help them with these skills, save to trust in their instinct.

I wanted to understand more about leopard communication, as non-verbal communication is a special interest of mine. As bats live in a world of ultrasound and snakes in a world of infrared, how did the cubs experience their lives in a world of super-sense and extra-sensory perception? Among the great mammals of the planet, whales communicate with the haunting and secret beauty of song, elephants rumble to each other in infrasonic sound, a register too low for the human ear to discern. Their messages are transmitted over vast distances, detailing the concerns of their migrations, of their bonding, their work songs and their greetings. What was the substance of leopards' silent communication?

Much is said about the 'sixth sense' of cats, or their extra-sensory perception. All cat lovers tell of times when their cat's uncanny ability or behaviour has stopped them for a moment, stunned by the illogicality of it and left them asking themselves 'What if?'. With leopards, so much is a mystery and so many questions remain unanswered. JV pointed out to me that leopard cubs will know when to stay put or when to follow at their mother's side. No matter how closely you watch a leopard family at a time like this, there is no 'follow me' flick of the leopard mother's tail, no sound or gesture from her to indicate her intentions. How do the cubs know what she wants them to do? Elmon looked surprised when I asked him his opinion. 'She tells them,' he said simply.

There are so many divergent yet co-existent worlds we live in as different species. What is the nature of the leopard's world? At the base of the pyramid, where the species differentiate, lie myriad consciousnesses, behaviours and communication styles. Yet at the apex, overarching it all, there is unity. Did this explain the curious sense of 'recognition' I felt sometimes in the presence of the cubs? How to find avenues into that collective state became a personal quest and I was happy for even the faintest glimpses of insight.

Relationships are systems which have components more than the sum of their parts. One of these was the inter-species communication between us, beginning with the provision of food and security, transforming at its highest level into an indefinable 'connection'. This was what I wanted to explore with Little Boy and Little Girl. I visited the cubs as often as I could to facilitate whatever pathways might open.

In the early days of sitting with the cubs, communication had been about revealing who we were. From there, we had moved to touching, letting the language of energy carry the communication deeper. I began to experiment in our 'meetings' with various improvisations, particularly with a technique of bodywork called 'the T-touch'. Linda Tellington-Jones developed this systemised form of touching, initially in her work with horses in the United States and later extending it to other animals. It involves various touches and degrees of pressure, all based on a gentle circular motion. The work can be used for healing, for calming and for communication. One works by focusing consciousness into the fingertips, clearing the mind and directing it singly towards connection with the other at the point of touch. As humans will hold another's hand when words are inadequate, would this technique facilitate communication between our two species where words were inapplicable?

I tried the technique on Little Boy and Little Girl for the first time when they were relaxed after a walk. In a brief session, they allowed me to massage light circles over almost their entire bodies. I carefully avoided the face and the head, which are ultra-sensitive, richly embedded as they are with touch receptors, and worked more towards the neck and down the flanks.

The cubs looked at me askance, their ears swivelling in curiosity as to what I was up to this time, but they showed no resistance. The next day they were in an alarmingly skittish mood, scratching and biting more than usual. I was afraid that I had been overzealous, that my therapy had backfired and thrown the cubs off-balance. Then again, a disturbance is often the beginning of progress.

I was hesitant about continuing, but encouraged by reported successes with T-touch, let Little Boy and Little Girl's responses guide me. There were days they clearly didn't feel like what I was doing and they indicated this by simply getting up and moving away. Sometimes I suspected they were indulging me, patiently tolerating my efforts. I interpreted that as a kind of progress. Then there were glorious moments when I felt we might just be sharing something. The cubs were tentatively participating in what I was trying to initiate.

Something worried me. Leopards are solitary animals that take their strength from solitude and silence. I regarded that as sacred, so I limited my mind-talking experiments to brief periods. Was I teaching the cubs and asking them to respond to me in ways contrary to their inner nature? These concerns filled me with uncertainty and I was drawn into an ongoing inner debate about the relentlessness of my human desire to want to know, to push the barriers. I have never resolved this issue within myself.

There were days too, when the cubs seemed so inaccessible – times when Little Girl's hostility was tangible, as if her thoughts were radiating in sharp spikes around her. Sometimes her resistance was more like a wall – solid and impenetrable. Strangely though, even in this negative space, I felt a connection with her. With Little Boy, good natured and tolerant, my attempts at mind-talking left me unable to connect at all, even though he was showing no obvious signs of resistance. Little Boy baffled me. When I did experience what I thought was a slight shift in his receptiveness, the door was never open for long and afterwards it felt like it hadn't happened. Was he asking me to collude in some way, suggesting that we could play these mind-talking games but then afterwards pretend that they had not happened?

It was the lack of clarity that frustrated me, rather than the lack of success. I eventually came to accept that, if the point of this relationship with Little Boy and Little Girl was to be about reciprocity, I had to be receptive to it in whatever form it came.

While doing this work with Little Girl and Little Boy, I'd consciously think of Mother Leopard, sensing her presence in the moment. I brought her into the situation via thought in this way, because I felt gratitude towards her. And hope. She had initiated the shift in my consciousness and in my ideas about leopards. I recalled the magical connection that was visible in the partnership between her, JV and Elmon. That connection was what I was trying to pursue for our team with Little Boy and Little Girl.

So often I'd appeal to her to facilitate what I was trying to do. After all, she had inspired me to find out what kinship with wild creatures meant and to discover how best to tread the path of reconciliation.

Even though I was not that close to Mother Leopard during her lifetime, I felt a strong resonance that remained after her death. It seemed as though the force of her spirit had set up a wave of energy, a morphic field where information resides and, as in a collective mind, becomes available to all life caring to tune into it. Here, perhaps, lay the essence of her experiences with humans, the pathway she had pioneered. Ultimately, what was it that I personally wanted to say to the cubs? I think it was something about being one of many humans wishing to relinquish dominance. To walk a path towards harmonious co-existence with all forms of life.

It was drawing near to the time of the feature film shoot, scheduled for the end of spring. The cubs would be six months old. Their usual routine was about to be disturbed and their familiar and comfortable ways disrupted. There was no way of knowing whether the cubs thought or projected into the future in the way that humans did, but I wanted to convey to them some idea of what was coming up. I wanted to reassure them that they could trust us to guide them safely through this big project we'd been called on to do together; they for leopards and us for humans.

The cubs were in a sleepy, relaxed mood that evening as I entered their boma. The paraffin lamps were glowing in the dark, their soft light falling in circles on the sand, the smell of burning paraffin hanging heavy in the air. Little Girl was lying on a high branch in their enclosure and she glared at me with her pupils dilated. In one cold moment, I understood that she was going to jump at my face. I tried to step back slowly while she was working up to her leap, but as I moved away, I felt the solid form of the tree trunk behind me, preventing me from moving any further. I was pinned against it. The wire mesh of the boma was at my other side, so there was no escape. I didn't want to traumatise her by shouting or hitting out at her. Neither did I want to be on the receiving end of her aggression. The inevitable recriminations would be a major setback to our relationship and to the project.

How fast one's mind can work. How much passes through it in a second when adrenalin and cortisol pump. I knew that before me lay either an opportunity or a disaster. Nothing in-between. I concentrated my mind as steadily as I could – there was no place for fear – and resisted the natural impulse to throw my hands up over my face in defence. Any sudden movement might cause her to react instinctively and I needed to reach her beyond the level of instinct. I tried to convey to her that I understood, but could not accept her aggression.

It was a long moment, in reality probably only a nanosecond, but there was distinct stuff passing between us. Little Girl was quite firmly in leopard mode and I quite definitely in human mode – in some corner of my mind terrified and not wanting my face shredded. I desperately wanted to avoid assuming the dominant position and, by sheer force, tyrannising her into obedience. I wanted Little Girl to choose, and to choose for our relationship.

As suddenly as I sensed the moment of her imminent attack, I sensed her change her mind. She climbed down the branch and flopped heavily onto her side on the sand floor of the boma in an exaggerated gesture. She let out the deepest sigh. Was it sheer exasperation?

I approached her tentatively and stroked her gently under her chin. She responded by rubbing her chin against my hand, giving herself to the moment. I stroked her in light circles, avoiding any intensity of thought, just letting the moment carry itself. I asked her for nothing that she was reluctant to concede. I knew that she was struggling between the duality of her two natures. I wanted her to know that I loved her unconditionally and that I understood her dilemma – whether to choose the path of pure leopard behaviour or whether to give herself over to the strange process that had put her life and that of humans on one path. I was willing to be there in whatever capacity she chose. I would provide her with food and security. I could be a friend if she wanted.

I circled around her chin, over the fine sharp bones of her cheeks, the sensitive areas of the sinus and around the ears, working over the reflex points with sensitivity and gentleness, offering goodwill. As I worked around the muscular parts of her neck and shoulders and down her flanks there was an unusual ease in her body, a sense of her receiving. It was so pure a moment, uncluttered and timeless. I used the opportunity Little Girl gave me to gently lift her lip and circle around the gum and mouth, that sensitive part of the predator where stress and tension is held and is expressed by sharply reactive biting, something Little Girl often did. The idea of the T-touch method is to diffuse that tension by short-circuiting the energy which is blocked there and letting it flow freely, using the human's energy system as a conduit. She allowed me to proceed.

An hour passed as we sat there and when I came out of the boma that night I was limping with pins and needles. I could hardly suppress my joy, for a moment of truth had passed between us. What the implications of this would be, I didn't know. I hoped that by giving herself over to trust, she would lose some of the anxiety she carried, which would be made worse by the heavy demands of the film shoot.

* * *

Leppie, the soft toy leopard, was in a sorry state. As the weeks passed, his tail was steadily bitten shorter and shorter. He was still a firm favourite. Little Boy particularly became possessive about his prize.

Karin was trying to get some shots of him as he lay sleeping outside the tent. She wanted to get a low angle and, needing to get down on the ground, cast around for something on which to steady her camera. Usually we use a 'low boy' tripod, or a beanbag, but none of the equipment was handy at the time. She saw Leppie lying close to Little Boy, where he had discarded him before falling asleep, picked him up and rested the camera on his back.

Little Boy woke up instantly and became agitated, circling Karin and making low moaning noises. At first she wasn't sure what the problem was and became concerned for Little Boy's health. Finally, she guessed and left him to see what would happen. Little Boy made his circles tighter until finally, he snatched Leppie from under the camera and restored him to his former sleeping place on the grass.

Karin underestimated Little Boy's obsession with Leppie and waited for him to doze off again so she could use Leppie to get her shot. He looked extremely fetching lying stretched out with his chin upturned, the picture of feline self-content. Again, Little Boy woke up and retrieved Leppie, without displaying the least bit of aggression, just a patient repetition of what he had meant the first time, as if she wasn't quite 'getting it'. Karin suppressed a smile and this time, when Little Boy repositioned Leppie where he wanted him, she respected his wishes, went off in search of a beanbag and continued her film work. Little Boy offered her no resistance. Karin got her shot.

We patched Leppie's disintegrating form as best we could to enable whatever existed between Little Boy and the toy to play itself out. With Leppie as the pivot, an interesting dynamic between Little Boy and Little Girl came to light. Little Girl bit off a piece of Leppie's fur. We saw her strutting through the camp with her head held high, the chunk dangling from her mouth. Her body talk was clearly that of one-upmanship and before too long, it drew its desired response. Little Boy was outraged and without much effort took her prize from her. Little Girl's face darkened with anger, her whiskers pushing forward. Flaunting *his* Leppie, Little Boy paraded up and down before her, squeezing every ounce out of the moment.

Little Girl brooded on this incident for some time and analysed the event from all angles. Some weeks later, she came up with an ingenious counter-strategy. She knew that she could never steal Leppie away from her brother with a direct attack. As Little Boy lay in his position of dominance – Leppie squashed down beneath his chest and forepaws – we saw Little Girl at the side of the tent. She was trying to create the impression that she was resting in the shade of the tent flap. Her body talk gave her away. She was strategising and feigning indifference as Little Boy lay there flaunting his prize.

Casually, she walked across to Graham who was sitting outside his tent and started attacking his sandal. He was wearing rubber thongs, which the cubs adored biting because of the chewy, rubber soles. Graham flicked the sandals off his feet to avoid having his ankles scratched, as Little Girl circled round and round, launching herself in a series of ferocious leaps and swats. Watching Little Boy from the corner of her eye, she overplayed her triumph in winning the thong, biting it and flipping it into the air with exaggerated abandon.

Her brother, unable to resist pirating anything from her, stood up, alert. In so doing he released Leppie from his front paws. Stage one of Little Girl's diversionary tactic was successful. On and on she went with the sandal, batting it this way and that, shoulder-rolling on it, pouncing on it and killing it time and time again.

Little Boy was caught. Down he went into a crouch. He pounced on Little Girl, knocking her away from the sandal. In two seconds she recovered her balance, flashed over to where Leppie lay and snatching him up with her front teeth, dashed off to a safe distance. There she flaunted him tantalizingly at her brother. Little Boy stood dumbfounded, the sandal dangling from his mouth, trying to work out exactly how he had lost Leppie.

Taking the cue from Little Girl, Karin good-naturedly teased Little Boy. She hid Leppie for brief periods and watched him trying to find him and work out who had tricked him. She wedged him into a tree one day. Little Boy moaned pitifully and ran backwards and forwards, looking for a way to climb the impossibly tall tree. Eventually, he scaled the scary heights of the tree to effect his rescue, his eyes blazing. He brought Leppie to the ground and stood over him for the rest of the afternoon defending him, alternately showing how offended he was about the whole affair and flashing accusing looks at anyone who came near.

Leppie's colleague, Lion, the other soft toy, had not fared as well. He was disembowelled as he hung from his rope in the cubs' boma, his clumps of white cotton innards scattered in a circle around his depleting form. The cubs used him for boxing practice, rising up on their hind legs and batting the surprised-looking Lion with one paw and then the other, as little wisps of stuffing flew from his body and floated lightly to the ground.

When the cubs became fascinated with our shoes and chewed them with a vengeance, we knew their teeth were loosening in their mouths and irritating their gums. They needed to bite on a 'teething ring'. We all pretty much gave up on wearing rubber sandals – a pity, as they were functional around the camp. Graham sacrificed his pair, tying one to the end of a pole, which he swung around. He drew a manic response from the cubs who hurtled after the thong, round and round the pole, leaping at it, cutting through the corners, trying to intersect it as the shoe suddenly came alive and flew around tantalizingly.

When the cubs first found the string floor mop they attacked it, enjoying sinking their claws and their teeth into the string. The mop was rejected after they tired of it. We put the forlorn mop into a new context. We took it out of camp, trailed it enticingly through the grass and wedged it up a tree. This caught the cubs' attention. They riveted their eyes on it with an expression of curiosity, trying to work out how their mop had escaped from the camp and found itself stashed up a tree.

Toilet rolls were a target for a while. The soft texture invited attack and the enticing way the paper snaked excited the cubs. Many times we had to go chasing after the cubs into the bush as they made off with yet another unravelling roll from our bush toilet. Exasperated, we secured the toilet roll on a hook much higher up the grass surround. But they outwitted us and found a way to steal the toilet roll by climbing the pole that supported the grass wall. And so on it went, with us trying to keep one step ahead and the cubs not far behind working out how to foil our plans. Or was it the other way around?

The first rains came after an overcast day in a drizzly, soft fall, bringing just enough moisture to wet the cubs' coats with droplets. Their eyes opened wide and their pupils dilated with excitement at this novelty. They shook off the water vigorously. Then, whatever it is about rain that turns cats silly, took effect. The cubs became energised, their behaviour skittish, and they chased each other this way and that, racing as if the devil itself were behind them. After a stretch of sideways galloping, ears pulled up backwards, they suddenly drew to a halt with a skid, or launched themselves at nothing in particular, landing in a heap, rolling uncontrollably over and over and then scrambling to right themselves before repeating the performance.

The big rains fell a week after that first shower. They came in a deluge characteristic of the lowveld region when the cycle of drought turns. First, the humidity builds to saturation point, then towards mid-afternoon, clouds roll in, billowing across the leaden skies and exaggerating the feeling of being pressed to the earth by the heaviness in the air. If the winds are favourable, gentle and blowing from the north, the rain will fall. This time it cascaded down in sheets. Within hours, the dongas came down in spate, the Inyatini and the Mashabene flowing like true rivers as the rain funnelled through the drainage lines from the catchments on the higher ground. The cubs were soaked to their skin, their flattened fur making their ears look overly large, and their little legs like pipe cleaners. For Little Boy it was as if he had found a kindred element, in the same way that Little Girl found hers when she first discovered trees.

After the drama of the first heavy falls of rain, the dongas drained, leaving some water trapped in pools in the rock piles at its edges. The sands of the floor were scoured smooth and clean. Little Boy could be found at this time sitting in the puddles with a silly expression on his face, or exploring the fascinating qualities of the water. He splashed in it, rolled in it, threw his body at it and skipped along the edges of the puddles in a frenzy, sending up virtuoso displays of water jets; or he would sit gazing at the ways the drops of water fell from the ends of his ears or dripped from the end of his nose.

While Little Girl was fascinated, it was clearly yet another learning experience for her. She was much more tentative about becoming famil-iar with the rainwater than her brother had been. She would only go ankle-deep and into the puddles, and as Little Boy became more and more enraptured, she would sit primly on the banks of the donga with her back held stiffly. Clearly, she was of a mind that his behaviour was excessive and inappropriate.

Towards the end of August, when the cubs were about five months old, there was a change. Little Girl shifted in some way. There was a new ease to her, a softness and a flowering of confidence, as in one who has moved from reluctance to acceptance. The most obvious signs were the control of her claws, which she retracted considerably when playing with us. She also stopped biting entirely; there was a less furtive sneakiness about her ways and she was less withdrawn. She didn't look so anxious and fragile anymore. The look in her eyes was different. Everyone in the team noticed. 'Yes,' they said, 'look how Little Girl has changed.'

Was it in dreamtime – so vital a part of every cat's life – that she had accessed guidance to help her understand the unusual path of her life?

\* \* \*

The dream was a recurring image. There she was, the old leopard, stand-ing with her head turned sideways, her eyes staring deeply, directly, so as to confirm the message that travelled from mind to mind on waves of energy. And there it was again, the almost imperceptible flick of the white tip of the tail, the 'follow me' sign that a mother leopard shows her cubs. She was standing on a pathway, her body talk inviting the cub to follow her. The path ahead of her was unlike an ordinary game trail, winding a path trodden by thousands of hooves, walking to and from the grazing areas to the sleeping areas and the waterholes. This path was the one humans used.

The leopard was an old female, her body frail. There was a cool energy about her and an aura of stillness. It was her eyes that remained in Little Girl's conscious mind long after the dream had faded. They were compelling eyes, ancient eyes, carrying a message: 'I have found a way.'

Little Girl blinked her eyes, as she started awake. She shook her head, half expecting the movement to settle the swirl of her thoughts. For an anxious moment, she scanned the bush looking for the leopard, but there was no movement, not a sound out of place, just the ongoing babble of the red-billed hoopoes in the leadwood tree. She drew in her hearing, isolating the interference, to concentrate more effectively. Her ears swivelled from side to side. There was no sound, no indication that what she had just experienced was present. But then, she had known that.

For weeks, Little Girl appeared as preoccupied as she was distressed. Was it the dream? A fragmented image of the half-forgotten image floated to the surface of her mind, recurring at unrelated times during the day. It touched at her consciousness, fleeting and unformed, then vanished. A half-focused idea would come to her and then slip away. *Mother*. Later, it came to her again like a soft sound, whispering, flickering at the edge of her mind, taking shape and then receding before she could fully grasp it. One day there it was. *Mother*. Little Girl still remembered the softness of her underbelly where she lay suckling as a cub, secure in her warmth, the throb of her pulse and the gurgling noises of life within her, the latent power in her muscles. But no, it wasn't her mother. The dreamtime mother was different.

With some hesitation, Little Girl took the dream to her brother. Little Boy reached for a solution when what Little Girl wanted was to be heard, to sense his sharing in her premonition. He rose to his feet and arched his back, feeling the full power of his muscles rippling through his body. He expanded his chest and drew his head slightly inwards, creating a menacing posture.

Little Boy had a plan. He would reconnoitre the area and seek out this strange leopard that kept appearing and disappearing. He knew exactly how to ambush her and drive her off. But Little Boy's courage was bravado. Inwardly, he was deeply afraid that his sister was in grave danger, for he knew two things. One, their mother was no longer with them and two, his sister was spending excessive time on mind work at the expense of developing her physical prowess.

Little Girl tried her best to hold onto the image of dreamtime, but the harder she tried to stabilise it, the faster it receded. Coincidentally, the same thing happened with the image of herself that she saw at the pond where she drank. At first, she was startled by her reflection in the water and drew back, but with her head bobbing slightly to see better, she approached the water again and tapped tentatively at the image. The harder she tapped, the more the image fragmented, dissipating outward into the water.

Daily as she drank, Little Girl watched her efforts at batting at the image come to nothing. Then, one day at Tortoise Pan, the place of the Great Fish Hunt, something happened. She was following a jacana, stepping long-toed from lily pad to lily pad with its angular but fluid movement. Not seeing her at first, the bird moved over the large circular water-lily pads that dotted the waterhole, pecking rhythmically at insects. Then, as it sensed it was being watched, it paused motionless, one leg raised. The ripples sent out by the slight rocking settled into stillness; the water lay undisturbed and the fragmented reflections consolidated to form a picture, just as a kaleidoscope of unrelated bits, given a moment of pause, settles and gels into a meaningful whole. As Little Girl watched the process, her mind moved.

Some days later, when the dream image of the female leopard touched the edges of her mind again, Little Girl let it float undisturbed in stillness, like the reflection of the water lily. And there it was, the mother leopard of Londolozi, standing on the path, her eyes beckoning. 'Follow me,' she said, 'I have found the pathway.'

The message was simple. It had been there all along.

\* \* \*

Little Girl lay in the middle of a thicket in ambush, her body bunched up, perfectly balanced, one front paw raised and curved slightly inwards in readiness. Her attention was focused on her brother who was ambling down the narrow path through the scented thorn woodland to his favourite pool. A slight rustling sound in a bush distracted Little Boy and he was curious to see what it was. He was half-heartedly investigating the noise when his attention was drawn away again, this time by a butterfly, which rose up from the grass and floated into the air. He concentrated on the butterfly's seemingly chaotic flightpath.

What luck! Her brother's diversion had put him right within her reach. She lowered her head and crouched behind a clump of grass, reading the moment perfectly. Hardly able to contain herself she froze, the pupils of her eyes dilating with the rush of adrenalin. Timing. Little Boy was entranced by the butterfly and, raised on his hind legs, was batting at it with his paws, still far too large for his squat body.

Little Girl pounced forwards, her front legs splayed stiffly, her hind legs providing the energy for the pounce. The perfect ambush. Little Boy leapt up in fright as his assailant flashed through the air, all four paws lifting from the ground simultaneously. Little Girl struck him mid-leap with her chest, knocking him clean off his feet. Together they rolled over and over together. Then, in a flash she extricated herself and shot through the undergrowth in headlong flight, ears flattened in mock terror at the counter-attack she knew would come as soon as her brother collected himself and recovered his dignity.

What a turn-around. Usually it was Little Girl that found herself being knocked over. Little Boy was no slouch. He bounded after her with good-natured vengeance. Together they zigzagged through the undergrowth, his superior strength allowing him to gain on her. Little Girl was the more nimble of the two and quicker around the corners. Again and again she outmanoeuvred him. Finally, in a desperate bid to even the score, Little Boy launched himself through the air with a massive leap, his lack of grace compensated for by his sheer power.

He landed right on top of Little Girl, flattening her to the ground and knocking the breath clean out of her body. She was not entirely spent though, and wriggling her body free, she mustered all her strength, rolled onto her back and raked at Little Boy's tummy with her hind legs, biting his ears with her razor teeth. Her brother rolled to avoid the rabbit-punching, pulling his head back into his neck and shielding his eyes, his ears flattened and protecting his throat from the biting frenzy in which he now, much to his surprise, found himself embroiled.

The strength of Little Girl's front paws was not equal to the power of the muscles in her brother's neck. He threw her off and bit into her neck.

The bite without his canines was largely ineffective, but with the power of his jaw he held tightly. For a moment the two combatants were locked in a stalemate of low and ominous growling, each playing for time, and in the pause, feeling for the slightest movement in the other which indicated a change of tactic.

Once they registered their impasse, they released their grip and lay side by side in the grass, panting. Little Girl rolled over her shoulder, lying upside down next to Little Boy, exposing the delicate white fur of her throat submissively, in a gesture of appeasement. Gently she held her brother's head between her front paws and licked his face. Little Boy wrinkled his nose but tolerated her grooming briefly. Then, he shook himself free and loped off nonchalantly, swivelling his ears to catch any early warning sounds of possible subversive plans Little Girl might have. There was an insouciant bounce to his step and swing to his hip; his body talk an expression of bravado.

Little Girl, with the feminine graciousness of victory, lay quietly in the shade of the trees, eyes half-closed with a smile of smug contentment. She knew that in the tussle, hers had been the superior tactics. Both she and Little Boy had the certain, if unspoken knowledge that it was she who had been triumphant. With her generosity of spirit, she had thrown the fight at the final moment, allowing her brother, whom she loved more than anything, to keep his ego intact.

# CHAPTER FIVE

# *Siyasebenza*

*We are working*

Melbourne, Australia, 3am – The telephone rang softly, made a slight whirring as the answering machine delivered its message, and then switched into fax mode in response to the incoming signal. Duncan McLaughlan turned over in his sleep and, registering the beep tone, made a mental note to check the in-tray first thing in the morning. As a film director, recently relocated from South Africa to Los Angeles and now temporarily in Australia, any communication coming at that time of night meant a long distance message, more likely than not to do with film work.

A simple note greeted him when he got up. 'Duncan, the mother leopard has been killed by lions. Are you available to make a feature film? Light and peace, JV.'

Duncan stood there in the early morning light, his mind reaching back through the years. An image came to mind. He was in JV's filming vehicle, an old Landrover, dented and scratched from years in the bushveld. JV was at the wheel, with Elmon following the leopard's tracks in the sand across a densely wooded, steep-sided gully. JV whispered, 'There, down below us with her cubs.'

Suddenly, a short growl, a flash of amber and ebony in a blur of movement only feet away from JV, who was sitting crouched on the hood, searching into the thicket. Topaz eyes glowed in the flickering shadow of a buffalo thorn bush. They scanned Duncan's face, their expression detached, yet penetrating in its intensity. JV scrambled back into the Landrover. And then silence. She was gone.

Duncan was at Londolozi directing JV in a film called *Silent Hunter*, a wildlife documentary about his and Elmon's struggle to film Mother Leopard, their long night vigils, their determination to tell her story on celluloid. He remembered JV saying that the two cubs with her, then about three months old, were her fourth litter.

As Duncan stood with the fax in his hand, a curious sensation passed through him. He remembered the aura surrounding this leopard, an otherworldly sense of mystery that he tried to capture on film. He recalled too the passion in JV to penetrate the secrets of her life. He had seldom worked with anybody so driven. What was striking initially about the mother leopard was her alluring beauty. It was a fierce kind of beauty, made all the more intense by her gentleness and tenderness with her cubs. And then of course there were her eyes, wise and compelling. They communicated some intangible message that he sensed but couldn't quite grasp.

In an instant JV's message had eclipsed the distance between continents and the intervening years. He smiled to himself and sighed. There was a sense of inevitability about it.

Londolozi, South Africa – Duncan sat on the veranda at the lodge, the scent of thatched grass tinged with the sweet smell of tamboti wood hung in the air. Eight years had passed. He could close his eyes and still be aware of the African bushveld; the characteristic clamminess of humidity; the heat; nature's rhythm in the sounds around him, the timelessness and stillness. From the ebony trees which shaded the veranda came the light twitter of masked weavers and the intermittent babble of a flock of red-billed wood hoopoes, their chatter started by one and taken up in chorus. 'Cackling women', the Shangaan call them.

September. Despite rain the bush remained dry, tawny with a fine layer of dust that settled everywhere. Before him stretched a vista of acacia thorn, leafless after the dry winter months and spectral against the late afternoon sun. He laughed out loud to see JV still driving the same battered film vehicle. How it had survived this long, he couldn't imagine, given the impossible job it did in the bush. He made a mental note to include the Landrover in the film he had come to Africa to make.

He and his partner Andrea, the scriptwriter, were grappling with some unusual problems. How were they to weave the fictional elements of the human drama around ten years of documentary footage? Mother Leopard's story, the main theme, was to be kept factual, for this film was primarily a tribute to her. Pre-production for the film had been a roller coaster ride so far, with most of the usually tidy sequence of events in the process of feature film-making happening back to front. Most notably, no leopard cubs, the stars of the film, had been forthcoming at the time the wheels of the project had started rolling. This made scripting and raising investment funding awkward. Then, at the point of desperation, as if by the presence of a guiding hand, two cubs from captivity in Zimbabwe appeared.

For Duncan, the process was an echo of his first experience of filming Mother Leopard with JV. Not much in that experience had gone according to plan or fitted into a schedule either. Instead of assuming his conventional director's role and controlling the story, he had found himself acting more as a conductor, trying to orchestrate an elusive melody, bits of which kept flying off at tangents while other unexpected refrains and chorus lines kept coming at him.

Casting the lead role was critical too if the film was to be successfully marketed to a wider international audience. They signed up Brooke Shields to star as the film-maker sent to Africa by a global television network. She was to cover the story of Mother Leopard and JV and Elmon's quest to save her newborn cubs after her death. Curiously, the auditions moved surprisingly smoothly. Brooke was to arrive that afternoon and there were still scripting issues to resolve. All the actresses who read for the part in Los Angeles were unfazed by working in hot, humid, malaria-infested locations in the African bushveld with untrained leopards. Perhaps it was the purity of Mother Leopard's story that appealed to them – the poignancy of an encounter where humans and animals strive together.

The sharp snap of branches and the rustle of leaves in the river bed below the lodge veranda brought Duncan out of his reverie. A small breeding herd of female elephants with their calves moved in slowly to feed on the greener foliage around the lodge. They ambled in to about 20 metres away, rumbling companionably to one another. There was a timelessness in their slow and deliberate movements, an awesome power in their presence. For Duncan, there was significance to the moment, a good omen perhaps for the film. These same elephant cows would have shared this bushveld with Mother Leopard. Who would know if they still held her in their legendary memories the way he did? Again, Duncan was aware of circles within circles and the sense of inevitability in his returning to Londolozi.

The film crew had moved onto location some weeks before, turning our quiet routine with the cubs and the gentle rhythm of our days on their head. Caravans and trailers littered the bushveld. Generators hummed and the film crew, unconcerned about harmonising with their environment, moved to and from film locations, laughing and shouting. This anticipation, bordering on hysteria, characterises the pre-production days leading up to a major film shoot. Bright and eccentric clothing blazed across the landscape, instead of the greens or khakis we wore to blend in with the shades of the bush. The high energy pushed the usual momentum of our days to a frenetic tempo. In an invisible circle surrounding T'Ingwe camp, a hush fell, as it had when we first moved into the bush to build the camp. The unseen inhabitants of the bush, once more rudely disturbed by or human goings-on paused, watched and waited.

A tree house was the main film set, built in the boughs of a large and gracious ebony a short distance along the donga. Most of the action in the film took place here, close to where the Inyatini joined the Mashabene, the heart of Mother Leopard's home range, where she had raised most of her cubs. Little Boy and Little Girl knew the area well from our repeated walks. We hoped that despite the intrusion of filming, their familiarity with the territory would give them confidence.

Quite strangely, neither Little Boy nor Little Girl was noticeably fazed by the sudden disturbance in their lives. Rather, they seemed intrigued. As preparations went ahead they hid under a tent flap, a table, or nearby bush, or up in the branches of the ebony, watching the activity on the film set with curiosity. We kept T'Ingwe camp itself free from filming, so that there would always be a sense of sanctuary. Should the cubs' nerves fail them during filming, they would have their boma back in camp as a bolt hole.

In the story, the tree house was JV and Elmon's base from where they went to film Mother Leopard in the lead-up to the near fatal lion attack on her at Parallel Clearing. Little Girl loved the tree house – the large platform high up in the ebony made intuitive sense to her and resonated comfortably with her affinity for trees. From there she had a 360-degree view of proceedings as the crew worked, giving her a sense of control over her fate.

In the screenplay, after Mother Leopard dies of her wounds, JV and Elmon rescue her cubs and keep them at the tree house. While raising them to independence, they search through Africa for an area to release the cubs, coming up en route against the obstacles of human bureaucracy, greed and the narrow scientific thinking which rules the lives of wild animals.

We were anxious that Little Girl and Little Boy would sense apprehension in a Hollywood actress and gang up on her in their well-rehearsed way. Even worse, we were nervous that they might scar her with scratches. Our calves and wrists were permanently cut from playing with the cubs. That's what it meant to engage with a leopard. They had fur to protect themselves in playful skirmishes and mock attacks, while our skin was exposed.

There is an industry that trains wild animals for films and generally those animals have their claws removed and their teeth filed. Little Boy and Little Girl were not trained animals and we were particularly mindful that their instinctive behaviour was key to their survival. In the meantime, it made for a spiky friendship.

The cubs behaved themselves beautifully when Brooke arrived on location. So much depended on a good rapport developing between them.

Brooke is a tall woman, which was helpful in that cats associate size with strength and have an innate respect for it. She was also confident with them and firm in her manner, which deflated their routine intimidation tactics. Brooke behaved sensibly around the cubs, not attempting to cuddle or smother them, being happy to get on with her acting and letting us deal with them. We ushered Brooke through the eight-week shoot with a few close calls and only a minor scratch to her leg. Little Boy did take it out on her shoes though, biting a sizeable chunk from the sole of her Doc Martin boots in what I thought was a smart piece of transference.

The film crew were briefed not to bend over or crouch near the cubs. This was an open invitation. Sudden movements around them would draw an instinctive retaliation. In particular, they were not to dangle fingers enticingly as when playing with a domestic cat. The urge to hold or stroke Little Boy and Little Girl was overwhelming. They were cute beyond words, but behind those large round eyes and those fluffy bodies was a wild, unpredictable nature. At stake was not only everyone's safety, but also the fragile trust we had created. The film crew were not to engage with the cubs at all, simply to behave like wallpaper around them. It was different for Brooke, as she needed to interact with them in the film for her role to be credible. All wild animals can see through pretence in a nanosecond, so Brooke had a challenging time acting her role and at the same time relating to Little Boy and Little Girl in a natural way, but from a safe distance.

With leopards, you never really know, but I'd like to think it was restraint on the cubs' part and, at an outside chance, that the Universe was on our side. Most likely, it was all of them. Karin and Graham's constant presence just out of sight of the cameras, hovering close by the action, hidden behind a bush or lying on an overhanging branch of a tree, offering bribes of snacks or waving the string mop, distracted the cubs from any malicious thoughts that might have strayed through their minds. Their job as handlers on set was to baby-sit Little Boy and Little Girl and to urge them to do what Duncan needed, or if not, then at least an approximation.

Their toys, Lion and Leppie, were still irresistible to them, battered and limbless as they were. Lion by this stage was entirely without stuffing and his plastic voicebox long gone. Both these toys were reincarnated as lures for the duration of filming. Karin and Graham assembled all the cubs' favourite toys in a special box that went on set each day. In addition to

Lion and Leppie, there was the mop, the rubber thong sandal dangling from the end of a stick, the impala tail and the dried palm leaf. All of these, to Little Boy and Little Girl's endless joy, would come alive at unpredictable moments and for no apparent reason, shake, rustle, leap or fly through the air, up a tree or behind a bush in a way no leopard cub could ignore. They would dash off after them in a frenzy.

Knowing Little Boy could never resist a snack, we stuck bits of meat in strategic positions on set when the toys failed to work their magic. To get her job done Karin had a flash of inspiration and produced a plastic container with chopped up meat snacks labelled 'cub grub'. The cubs soon came to know their box intimately and followed it around wherever it went. The sound of a stick tapping on the container was Pavlovian music to their ears. In this way we brought the cubs into position on the film set or off it, as called for by the script.

Animals used in feature films or other performance are trained using a system of positive and, sadly, negative reinforcement, with the trainer assuming a position of dominance over the animal to coerce its cooperation. It is a false perception of dominance, as the big cats are infinitely superior in strength to any human. Cats are, however, obedient within their own social systems to a hierarchy of perceived strength. By playing this mind game, animal trainers bluff cats into an artificial hierarchy to get them to do what is asked of them.

Because Little Boy and Little Girl were 'untrained', Duncan needed to be lateral in his way of working. Instead of trying to control the action, he improvised and set up an approximation of the shot he wanted. With the cubs lured into position with the cub grub container or one of the toys, he let the scene unfold spontaneously. This required some fast foot and finger work from the camera crew, who were familiar with more malleable and predictable human actors. Often, what Little Boy and Little Girl delivered was more creative than anything we could have scripted. Who knows, after all, what collective unconscious they were tapping in to for creative guidance?

While the crew was mostly adaptable, I did cause raised eyebrows when I suggested that Little Boy and Little Girl be included in the film credits with co-creating the script. After all, what could be more authentic than input into the action by genuine leopards?

As filming progressed, the cubs emerged with distinctively individual styles. Little Boy was particularly good at the more energetic shots where extravagant gesture was called for, plainly known as ham acting. He was required to knock Brooke off her hammock as she lay there, gently perspiring in the African heat, writing postcards home. Graham hid behind the tree trunk, dangling the string mop so that it danced around, inviting attack. Little Boy launched himself in a magnificent leap from the roof of the tree house and sailed through the air. He landed right on target, inches from Brooke on the hammock, swinging it back and dislodging her onto the floor in an undignified heap. His performance earned him a round of spontaneous applause from the crew.

Little Boy loved the limelight and basked in the glory and admiration of being a film star. He positively beamed after performing the way Duncan wanted and glowed when the crew cheered him. He felt the approval in their tone and the sudden lifting of energies that comes with capturing a successful shot. While he loved the approval, he loved even more the seemingly endless supply of rewards from the cub grub box. At the end of a shooting day, his tummy more often than not was distended with all the meat he had eaten. His basic good nature and buoyant temperament made Little Boy easy to work with and his comical antics on set made him a favourite with the film crew.

With Little Girl it was different. I always sensed in her some kind of inner conflict, as if by associating with people she was transgressing a basic law. The resistance I sensed in Little Girl touched me deeply. I supported it, admiring the purity of it. What after all were leopards' experience of humans historically, if not one of hostility? In the early days Little Girl had been unrelenting. Then had come the time when her defensive behaviour changed so dramatically. In some mystical way she had come to understand and more than that, to accept the task that was facing her even though she didn't ever fully buy into relating to humans. This showed in the mysterious way in which Little Girl worked. When called on to perform, she would assess the situation, keeping the crew waiting, and then perform some action so perfectly and so brilliantly understated. But she would do it only once and nothing would tempt or induce her to do a second take. If the crew missed the shot, it was gone forever. Afterwards, she would lie in the shade and groom herself in a self-satisfied way, without triumph or grandstanding as with Little Boy.

Neither of the cubs liked to be handled and once they were fed-up with film work, that was it. Or in the case of Little Boy, once he had eaten his fill. This prima donna attitude made nonsense of film schedules and constant rescheduling became the norm. The cubs performed in the morning and the evening, but in the heat of the day they would lie up in the shade. It was about the only thing we were able to predict about their performance during the film shoot.

The vernal equinox of September came and went, bringing with it the vigour of spring. As with autumn this is a brief interlude in the African bush calendar. Too soon the days became hotter and more humid. The early rains settled the dryness and dust of winter and, as the air became balmy, trees and shrubs flushed with the luminous green of new leaf. Buds burst between the thorns of the acacias and shoots of new growth emerged from the tangle of dry grass. Cream-coloured flowers appeared on the cubs' favourite tree, the russet bush willow. This sudden change in the tree's appearance drew curious looks from the cubs and enticed Little Boy into its branches to swipe at the blossoms. He stared in amazement as they parachuted lightly out of his reach to the ground below.

At six months old, the cubs had developed a slightly different expression in their eyes, one that spoke of a growing independence. In Little Boy this manifested in a slight cockiness, taking chances with us in his ambush play that were bolder and even cheekier than before. In Little Girl it enhanced the air she carried of a deeper knowing. Little Boy became more focused in his behaviour. He became more single-minded and his intentions clearer. Endearingly, he remained easily tempted with a snack. Happily though, his growing ability to concentrate was the early emergence of the focused thinking so essential for hunting and other tasks. His skills, mental and physical, needed to mesh and gel when his mind called for it.

Both cubs had shed their woolly coats, revealing sleek fur. A deep russet colour and burnished gold shone through the ebony rosettes marking their back and flanks, the fur on the legs spotted and the underbelly remaining pure white. As their adult teeth grew, the cubs chewed energetically on anything and everything to ease the itchy discomfort of their gums. The rubber soles of shoes remained a favourite. Wild leopard cubs chew on branches, but Little Boy and Little Girl had Brooke Shields' boots.

As they grew, their expressions became more varied and often comical. They wrinkled their noses in distaste when it drizzled, or flattened their ears when the wind threw the ambient sounds around haphazardly. It was a perfect time to be filming. Capturing these expressions in close-up shots gave the film the particularity of character that made the cubs so engaging, certain to win the hearts of audiences.

Leopards almost always deflect physical aggression, going to great lengths to avoid a confrontation, except in the most flagrant violation of their social arrangements. This was why Little Boy's behaviour the night we screened the rushes was so peculiar. 'Rushes' are sent back to the director on location as soon as film sequences have been processed in the laboratory. It helps the technical crew and the performers to review their work before moving on with the schedule. The first set of rushes reached us late one afternoon, shortly after we began shooting. As with most work in the bush we had to improvise – we strung up a sheet as a screen at the tree house.

As soon as it was dark, Duncan called to view the rushes. Little Boy had been a superstar that day. His modus operandi was to select a comfortable spot on the roof to rest. When he was needed on set, Karin tapped the cub grub bucket. Little Boy took up his position, did his bit, then returned to lie on the roof again, much in the way a human film star relaxes in a caravan or trailer between takes. He was still lying on the roof when the rushes arrived for viewing.

As the images rolled onto the makeshift screen – a sequence of Little Boy and Brooke – we heard a menacing growl behind us. Little Boy dropped into a crouch in response to this foreign leopard. He laid his ears flat and started snaking his head up and down, the way leopards do in full battle. The sheet was billowing slightly in the wind, making the screen leopard even more threatening as it moved. Magnified to such a size, the image scared him witless. He hissed, flattened his ears even further, then hurled himself at the screen, trying to swat at the image projected there.

As the leopard ran across the screen and out of frame, the real life Little Boy dashed after it into the wings. Then another image appeared, this time running directly at him. He lunged at it, smacking it ferociously and then as that image disappeared, Little Boy hurtled off after it. He was disconcerted when the screen leopard finally disappeared but was not dissuaded. He dashed behind the screen to look for his opponent there and not finding him, slunk around, sniffing the area for traces of the intruder.

Not even the helpless laughter from the film crew distracted him from his quest. Even though he was unable to find the aggressor, he seemed satisfied that his mean resistance had chased the trespasser off and shown that he was not to be pushed around in his own territory. Then, with great dignity, Little Boy resumed his position on the roof and, after some moments of thought, had a good wash.

Sometimes only Little Boy would be taken to the shoot, and Little Girl would be left behind in the boma. This made her nervous and stressed and she would call for him piteously. Nothing could distract her. If one of us stayed with her in the boma it relieved her stress slightly, but it was clear she was waiting for Little Boy's return.

Once, we let her out of the boma and she picked up her brother's tracks, by then some hours old, and followed him. There were several tracks laid on the ground around the camp, yet she was able to identify his most recent tracks – the ones that were most important to her. After a separation like this, she would stay very close to Little Boy on his return and sleep right next to him that night.

Often I would stay with her. The times we spent together then were for me the most precious moments during my time with the cubs. I tried to help sooth her agitation with a low voice, approaching to touch her only after some time had passed. Then I did bodywork with her and she would relax. I breathed with her and focused my consciousness at the point of touch where our individual energy fields merged. The communication was closer to feeling than to thoughts. It was about sharing the present moment. It was possible for two species, historically aggressive, to be safe within that space.

Sometimes my focus would slip and I would find myself momentarily in the role of the observer. The fragile connection between us would lapse briefly. I could only put my wavering down to the intensity of the experience. Tenuous as it was, it stretched my senses, my perceptions and challenged all paradigms. It was scary to discover in a wild creature the 'self' part that remains constant and stands separate from its physical form.

I tried not to let these moments of hesitation intrude as they distanced me from what I had come to call 'the zone'. They made me a spectator when the Universe was offering me the opportunity to participate in this wonder. For in these moments of empathy, I could understand in a fragmentary way what it meant to be a leopard, so extending the glimmer of this insight I had from Mother Leopard. With Little Girl, I sensed the incredible sweetness of her inner nature, so gentle and affectionate beneath the seriousness with which she regarded her role of being a leopard.

There were times of blockage when I hardly met her at all. These were usually at times when she was so stressed and agitated by her containment in the boma that her distress seeped into my own soul.

She expressed this frustration by pacing up and down along the fence with a vacant expression. Keeping the cubs enclosed in a boma had been an unhappy compromise. None of us was comfortable seeing the cubs contained but we lacked the skills of vigilance and the intuition that a mother leopard could provide in protecting her young.

My understanding of what captivity does to a wild animal, particularly a big cat, is that it causes a slow but sure dislocation of its psyche. Its instinct for physical survival will force it to comply with its captivity, often seemingly comfortably. But the cat's spirit of wildness cannot be contained and to escape the trauma of confinement, its spirit takes flight. Symptomatic of this psychic distress is a robotic pacing up and down behind the bars of the cage, as the restless physical body seeks to vent its pent up energy, while the dullness in the eyes reflects a soul that has fled. Watching a cat in this condition causes me deep anguish and reminds me of the rocking of an autistic child.

There is inevitable astonishment when a captive wild cat turns on and attacks its beloved keeper. I am sure that even the cat is alarmed by its own behaviour. I understand it to be a reaction of reflex, entirely on the physical plane, when its higher self no longer moderates the animal's behaviour – its soul having 'split off' as the Shamans would say, to defend itself from a living death.

When I saw Little Girl begin this mindless pacing, I intervened right away. I ran to her, scooped her up, supporting her under her body and chest from behind as if in a sling, leaving her limbs and her head free. I knew she hated being picked up yet it brought her consciousness fully into present time. Having broken the somnambulant rhythm of her pacing, I set her down again and withdrew to nurse my scratches. She lay down in the far corner of the boma, glowering at me with fury and then displaced her energy in a frenzy of grooming.

Later we found that simple distraction was effective in stopping the cubs from pacing. We arranged an obstacle course in the form of a series of sticks wedged at different intervals and heights through the mesh wire of the boma. This interrupted the rhythm of the pacing by forcing the cubs to overcome the hindrances in their path. The mind, being called on to solve tasks, could no longer separate itself from the present moment and drift off elsewhere.

The truly bizarre nature of our human technology was thrown into sharp relief when the cubs unwittingly tangled with it. They found the coiling and writhing of the electrical cables used to bring power onto the film set irresistible. They had us on our toes preventing them from biting through them and shocking themselves. The electronic buzz coming from the lights made them deeply suspicious and the generator that provided the power was a constant source of worry, especially when the engine pitch altered slightly. With nervous sideways glances, the cubs would crouch low and scurry past the generator truck, suspecting something alive and threatening was inside.

There were moments when, for no clear reason, either Little Boy or Little Girl would stop what they were doing, walk up to the camera, peer into the lens and lick it or bat at it, especially when we were angled at their eye level. Either that, or they would tackle the cameraperson. I took this as their way of saying it was enough filming for the day and respected their wishes. I worked in front of cameras during my TV broadcasting days and know the sense of invasion one feels. In cat language, a direct and ongoing stare means a challenge. Magnified and exaggerated by the size of the lenses, it must have been disconcerting for the cubs to be looked at intensely in this way. I always felt grateful to the cubs when they overrode those instincts and allowed us to get a shot. It felt like a generous gesture.

Nothing had prepared the cubs for the audio tape recorder. Prior to the feature film shoot we checked sound recordings by replaying them through headphones. In this way no one but the operator was disturbed by the sound. This was not the way sound technicians always worked on feature films though.

Shooting on set was going well. Duncan called for a break to rehearse the next few sequences. The technicians always used these opportunities for quick quality checks on their work. The make-up artist ran in with powder and puff, the hair stylist with comb and brush, the costume designer fiddled away with tucks and pleats and the camera assistants blew imaginary dust from lenses and load film.

The scene involved complicated camera angles and Duncan was in discussion with the lighting cameraman. In the screenplay, Elmon and JV are out in the bush while Brooke is relaxing in her hammock in the tree house, writing postcards. Little Boy and Little Girl are making her life difficult by chewing her letters and running off with her pen. It was a reasonably calm moment on the set with emotional temperatures unusually moderate for a feature film. Karin was concealed in an overhanging branch with the cub grub container.

Suddenly, the most awful volley of hissing and spitting erupted. Little

Girl came reversing across the tree house platform, her fur raised, her body enlarged to twice its size and her ears drawn flat. Little Boy exploded across the set in headlong flight as he swerved through lights and cameras, making the most urgent getaway. His fur was also raised and ears drawn flat, a look of blind panic in his eyes. He careered into a table, sending a bowl of nuts flying through the air. People ducked and chaos broke out as he scrambled across the set, skidding on the nuts now rolling all over the floor.

Everyone expected a snake to drop out of the tree or a lion to charge from the bush. Karin and Graham ran after the cubs to protect them. JV and Elmon leapt forward, rifles raised to confront the danger.

Nothing happened, except for a stunned silence. After a while, Little Boy emerged from his hiding place behind the pots and pans, tentatively edging forwards. All gazes followed him. What had scared him so? Slowly, using the cover of the set dressing of a couple of pumpkins lying on the floor, he moved cautiously towards the sound technician standing stooped over his tape recorder, and eyed him accusingly.

'Oh!' said the sound technician, looking up and smiling weakly. 'It must have been the tape replay.'

In the break he had been checking a recording of a leopard fight sequence. The sound of this played at high speed in reverse, as he looked for his sound cue was the source of the terror.

Little Girl escaped up a tree where she sat, giving us dark looks. Nothing would induce her to come down for rest of the day. Little Boy couldn't concentrate on his acting. He was keeping low to the ground, creeping cautiously from cover to cover, on guard for the assailant whose growling and spitting he'd heard nearby. And once again Duncan had to reschedule his shoot as there were no leopard performers available.

About halfway through the feature film shoot, Little Boy did something contrary to his nature that had us all nonplussed. He was strolling amiably among the crew as they set up a shot in the tree house. The scene involved Brooke conning a nature conservation official who had come to confiscate the cubs.

Di, the continuity person, was on set, marking her script in preparation for the shoot. She noticed Little Boy walking towards her and thought nothing of it. According to Karin, who was minding him that day, there was no hint in his body talk or in his expression that he intended to do what he did next.

Little Boy continued towards Di, stopped immediately in front of her and examined her legs closely for a good few moments. Di stood quite still as instructed to when the cubs were around. She was wearing leopard-print leggings, and it crossed her mind that it might have been the print that intrigued Little Boy. Then, he simply opened his mouth and bit down hard on her calf, drawing a stream of blood.

Di yelped, more with shock than with pain. We thought that our worst fears were being realised and the predictions of the doom prophets were about to unfold before our eyes. Our untrained leopard was about to maul a human being.

But he didn't do that. Instead Little Boy leapt back in alarm, surprised as anyone by the fuss around him and by Di's reaction. He sat there looking at us with a quizzical expression, cocking his head from side to side. Fortunately for Di he was still without his upper canines, the first one having fallen out some months before and the second lost in the Leguvaan Battle.

I knew that Little Boy hadn't mistaken Di for a leopard. That would have been an insult to his intelligence. I was left wondering in amusement though, whether his prank was some kind of comment on her fake leopard fur outfit and what he might have seen as her attempt at cross-dressing.

For some reason, Little Boy and Little Girl relocated the remains of Lion, their toy, to a spot in the donga away from the camp. When there was any time off from film work, they'd head off and ritually maul Lion. A form of film star stress release? Lion was virtually decapitated, his head hanging on by a thread, but this did not concern the cubs. They pounced at him from the cover of the riverine shrub in a repertoire of leaps, twisting and arching athletically through the air, landing on top of him from different angles, swatting at him and rolling over him vigorously, scooping up his tattered body with their front paws and thrusting him up into the air, trying to force him to respond.

Leppie, unfortunately, had simply disappeared. We suspected that one of the cubs had stashed him in a tree somewhere and forgotten where. This shows just how ignorant humans can be. A leopard never forgets the location of its larder. The film crew accidentally locked Leppie in the props trunk. When the props assistant held him up with an exclamation of joy, Little Boy streaked across the film set, snatched him up in his jaws and dragged Leppie to the same spot in the donga where Lion lay. Here he released Leppie in the sand and went about ritually killing him.

Thinking he'd reinstate Leppie in the trunk of equipment used for luring the cubs on set, Graham fetched the toy from the donga. From nowhere and once again as straight as a bullet, Little Boy shot across the set, snatched Leppie up between his teeth and dragged him off to the same spot in the donga, the 'killing field'. Leaving him there he returned to camp, glaring at Graham reproachfully.

Little Girl had given up taunting her brother with Leppie, so fixated was he on the toy, except once when she snatched his remains and dashed up a tree. From his new favourite position on the palm leaf roof of the vehicle carport, Little Boy spotted her and in two bounds was after her. He retrieved Leppie so rudely that in snatching the toy he accidentally bit off and swallowed Leppie's tail. He had to eat plenty of grass before he managed to vomit it up.

The cubs were growing fast, and their physical abilities were maturing. Frisbee became a great hit. As we threw the plastic disc from one to another in a circle, Little Boy and Little Girl demonstrated a range of fantastic leaps. Little Girl was a master at the game and an excellent jumper. She was also far more willing to let go of the frisbee once she had caught it, understanding that we'd throw it again for her. Little Boy didn't quite trust this process, so when he caught it he would bite down on it hard (at this stage, still with his gums) and run off with his prize into the donga or onto the roof of the tent. His sense of play expressed itself more comfortably in the tree-bouncing games, where there was no object to possess. When the frisbee was around, or the soccer ball or Leppie or Lion, it was a serious challenge to his dominance when anyone messed with the object.

During film work, there was only a single incident when the offer of a snack of meat from the cub grub box failed to attract Little Boy. A dummy leopard was brought onto the film set from the taxidermist, fully dressed in real leopard skin. The dummy was used for sequences in the film that were too risky to shoot using the cubs. Either they would be in danger, as with the scene where they interact with a large male lion, or we ran the risk of having Brooke or another actor scratched.

Duncan enjoys creating tense moments in his high-action films. There was always a chance that the untrained cubs would react defensively in the excitement of the moment and injure someone. There were sequences in the film of the tree house erupting in flames, of helicopter and aeroplane battles and frantic high-speed chases across the bush in the

Landrovers. The cubs were filmed in sequences leading up to the event or capturing close-up shots of their reaction to the moment and then substituting the dummy.

Little Boy had his own agenda with the dummy leopard. The moment he saw it, and it was from at least 50 metres, he stalked it briefly then flashed across the set before anyone realised what he was up to. He tore into the stiff and lifeless dummy with ferocious growls and then dragged it, all four limbs stuck stiffly in the air, to the tree house platform. He released it, then pounced onto its back. He bit first at its spine and then, grappling with his front paws to secure his hold on its body, he went straight for the throat.

We stood back, astounded at this killing technique that predators usually have to learn. Little Boy seemed to have got it down pat in his first go. Perhaps it was the practice with Little Girl in their games, more likely because the lifeless dummy put up no resistance. I was lost in admiration at Little Boy's achievement, while being a little concerned that he hadn't first assessed the potential threats to himself.

The film crew was in a panic. The dummy had cost thousands of dollars and was about to be ripped into shreds by the cubs who by now were completely out of control. A deep instinct in them had been unleashed. Little Girl, after weighing up the situation, circled around, using the cover of the furniture on set, and then leapt into the fray.

In the melée, someone pulled the dummy from Little Boy. His eyes glowed, his ears pulled flat and he growled as he sank to the ground deeply and menacingly, in preparation for pouncing at the person who had dared take his prize. Fortunately it was Karin who, realising the danger, flung the dummy over the platform to the ground below where one of the crew picked it up, hurled it into the props trunk and shut the lid smartly.

The cubs hurtled down the swing bridge, pawing at the trunk and leaping on it in fury. Some time passed before they calmed down. First they circled the trunk suspiciously and then lay next to it, guarding it while regarding the crew with hostility. The sight of the dummy was the initial spark, but it was the scent that enraged them. The scent was still prevalent to the cubs, although the animal had been dead a long time and a taxidermist had treated the skin with chemicals.

That was the end of film-making for the day, despite much tapping of the cub grub box and waving bits of meat around to lure them back to work. There was no distracting them from the mission of tracking down this new interloper. This time both of them knew for certain by the scent still lingering in their nostrils that their foe was a real leopard.

For a while after the incident we had an effective new method of luring the cubs back to T'Ingwe camp when they were reluctant to return. This new dummy leopard lure especially pleased Graham, still sore from his session of some six hours under a tree at dusk, waiting for Little Girl to complete her communing before he could finally get her to the safety of the boma. There was a risk attached to this particular lure. Once it was out of the trunk and the cubs saw it, you had to run like a fury. They would leap at your chest and swipe at your ankles to trip you and force you to drop the dummy.

During their film work, the cubs learnt about some of the more dangerous creatures they would encounter later in the bush and how to interact with them. This was the case with the snakes we brought onto set, the trained lioness and the porcupine.

There is a sequence in which the cubs were discovered unprotected in their rocky lair, while their mother is out hunting. A lioness sniffs them out and digs menacingly, trying to get at the cubs. For Little Boy and Little Girl hiding in the rocks, it was terrifying to see the lioness's huge head looming in at them. Her glowing eyes spoke of murderous intent, made all the more menacing by her digging paws and her sniffing. It was hard for us to watch this scene. How 'right' their instincts were, even though they had no wild leopard mother to guide their behaviour.

In an attempt to avert the lioness 'attack', they flattened their bodies to the ground and froze, relying on the safety of their lair to protect them. Had they bolted in the wild, the lioness would have been on them in seconds and killed them. We were able to get a credible shot for the film, but more importantly, to expose the cubs to a real lion which allowed them to experience its scent and sound.

The scene with the python was hilarious. Little Boy didn't see it at first, so well camouflaged was the snake's mottled skin against the base of the dappled sycamore fig. The snake handler was standing by, more anxious about his python being bitten by the leopards than the snake biting them. We were wary of the lightning speed with which a python coils its body around its prey. You can only stop this process by killing the snake.

In this sequence, JV is filming Little Boy playing around in the exposed roots of the tree, when they come across the python.

The snake sensed the warmth of Little Boy's body or his movement, for it began slithering and coiling in the root system of the tree. Little Boy tried to snarl bravely, managing only to look comical and not at all intimidating without his canines. As the rush of flight adrenalin got the better of his courage, he leapt back, rising in an undignified four-legged leap into the air. He landed awkwardly in the roots, slipping and scrabbling wildly, but untangled himself and fled so quickly, seemingly without touching the ground.

The porcupine is Africa's largest rodent. It defends itself by backing up against its aggressor, protecting all the vulnerable parts of its body with the sharp, pointed quills on its back. At the base of its tail are particularly vicious quills which it rattles antagonistically, enhancing the intimidating effect of its spiky appearance.

An inexperienced predator usually comes off second best in these counter-attacks, with quills stuck through its paws or cheeks, difficult to remove because of the barbed hook at the tip. The quills cause an open infected wound, which can be fatal. Determined predators learn the highly specialised hunting technique of flipping a porcupine over and attacking the soft underbelly, but the technique takes time and practice to perfect.

Little Boy, when set against a porcupine for a film sequence, characteristically went for the direct approach. He launched himself at the porcupine, only slightly put off by the rattling of its quills. Recklessly, he swiped at it with his paw and then, shot with quills, he jumped back and hid in the thicket, wide-eyed, trying to work out what had happened. Little Girl was more circumspect, watching her brother. The unscathed porcupine made its getaway by swimming across the dam. Little Boy sat in the bush tugging at the quills that were stuck in his paw with his teeth. Six had pierced right through and were so securely wedged there he could not remove them.

In the film, as the cubs are nearing an age where they need to be released into the wild, JV and Brooke uncover a plot to steal the cubs and sell them to animal traders dealing in exotic fur. Brooke distracts the villain while JV and Elmon make a dramatic escape with the cubs in a light aircraft. After a daredevil stunt and some exciting aerobatics, JV flies off, with the cubs peering poignantly out the window. They flee Londolozi and escape to the Maasai Mara in Kenya, where JV appeals to his Maasai friends for sanctuary.

Formerly, the Maasai were a nomadic people, following the rains and pastures that created their migratory patterns. The courage of the Maasai is legendary. Their folklore abounds with tales of morani* fighting off

*morani: warriors

lions armed with only a spear and a rungu*. Their relationship with leopards is a troubled one. At night, leopards are known to break through the mud walls of their manyattas*, to prey on the young calves sheltering within. While the Maasai respect the stealth and intelligence of leopards, such an unseen and unpredictable enemy evokes animosity.

Because of this history, the tribal elders eyed Little Boy and Little Girl with deep suspicion when they arrived in Kenya for filming. It was only our longstanding friendship with the Maasai of the Kyoki branch and the respect the elders have for JV that persuaded them to participate in our film project. That and some good cash bargaining.

The Maasai are a cultural hybrid, steadfast about many traditions yet yielding in others to encroaching western ways. Tourists visiting Kenya are awe-struck by their beauty, and the morani are very much aware of their own physical magnificence. So the Maasai have turned picture-taking into a lucrative business.

Out of storage came their finery and traditional gear, the ostrich feather headdresses and the lion manes. Exquisitely woven ceremonial beads were draped around their necks and looped through their ears. Brightly coloured shukas* blazed red across their handsome bodies.

The shoot went magnificently, until the day Little Girl misbehaved herself and came within an inch of being killed by a furious Maasai warrior, brandishing his spear and rungu.

The scene was to be shot inside the Maasai manyatta, a cluster of mud and thatched huts grouped roughly in a circle, surrounded by a fence of thorn branches to protect the cattle and goats at night. The action involved many Maasai warriors, women and children. Their herds of cows and goats were needed too, so on the morning of the shoot they were all held back in the manyatta instead of going out to graze in the fields. With all the extras, there wasn't much space. Amid all the excitement no one was paying much attention to instructions, so it was taking a while to get the shoot started. Warriors milled around admiring themselves and each other, cattle and goats were lowing and bleating, disturbed by the change in their routine and in their confusion bumping into camera and lighting equipment. The crew grabbed left and right to save gear from falling over while trying simultaneously to set up.

When the cubs were brought on set in their travelling cage, their arrival was barely noticed. Believing they were secure in the box, Karin and Graham were temporarily distracted as they tried to find out exactly what

*rungu: club *manyattas: groups of huts *shukas: toga-like cloths it was Duncan wanted from them for the scene. Little Girl somehow slipped out of the travelling box and with great concentration, began to stalk a goat. Using the people bustling around as cover, she edged her way quietly around the boma and then, when she was within striking range, crouched low and stared at the goat with her best intimidating glare, a bit perturbed that it didn't bolt. The goats meanwhile, scared witless by the sudden presence of a leopard among them, froze on the spot. Then one of them made the fatal mistake of turning its back on Little Girl. She pounced at it, sinking her claws into its back. The goat bleated in shock and leapt into the air bucking and kicking with Little Girl hanging onto its back, using her weight to twist its neck and force it to the ground before making the killing bite to the throat.

Duncan and JV, opportunistic about grabbing shots, shouted instructions to the cameramen, 'Roll, roll, roll!'. Karin and Graham were mortified that they had slipped up in their jobs and that the cubs had escaped. Along with the trunks packed with props that travelled to Kenya went the special box of the cubs' toys. They threw their rubber-thronged sandals at Little Girl and alternately swiped at her with the string mop and the cub grub bucket. Dust flew everywhere, cow dung scattered in clods and the rest of the goats and the cattle began to panic, stampeding into each other and everything else. Little Girl's prey continued bucking, putting up a fierce resistance while Little Girl hung doggedly on to its back, her eyes blazing. A goat rodeo. In its effort to escape, the goat stumbled into one of the tripods, sending a camera and the director of photography sprawling to the ground.

That was when Ngodella, one of the Maasai warriors with a lifetime of believing that problem goats should be speared, quietly raised his spear and moved towards Little Girl, his rungu ready in his other hand. Fortunately, JV saw Ngodella moving stealthily across the back of the scene and flung the bag he was carrying at Little Girl, managing to dislodge her from her prey just in time before Ngodella thrust his spear. The young herdboys rescued the goat and the crew captured Little Girl, who was totally confused by the loud objections surrounding her brilliant first hunt.

After the chaos settled there was a prolonged hush in the manyatta, followed by an outbreak of vociferous complaints. The elders demanded compensation. It took time and diplomacy to settle the issue and once again, Duncan was left to reschedule the shoot he'd planned. The cubs, extremely pleased with events, remained in a highly elevated mood, hurtling through the bush after scrub hares for most of the afternoon.

A huge full moon rose out on the clearing that night, alongside the film crew's tented camp. It hung low and yellow on the horizon before edging its way slowly into the sky. For a while the cubs stayed out of their boma in the cool evening air, enjoying the openness of the savannah. Little Boy lay still, staring at the night sky, perhaps puzzling over the slightly different configuration of stars. Little Girl kept rolling over and over on her back. It looked for all the world as if she were laughing.

The wrap of filming in Kenya signalled the end of the feature film shoot. The production crew and actors all moved off from Londolozi and the film went into post-production in Johannesburg. There were still pick-up shots to be done with the cubs but we would do these ourselves later.

A hush descended over T'Ingwe camp and the tree house once the crew moved off, leaving us shell-shocked after eight frenetic weeks. We soon settled into our former rhythm of walking with the cubs in the early mornings and evenings.

It was the summer solstice in the southern hemisphere and nearly the end of the year, deep into the wet cycle of the seasons. The heat, intense with humidity, rose to saturation point, bringing a dampness and heaviness to the air.

The good rains encouraged the trees to flush their canopies of leaves. While providing shade, they offered little relief from the humidity. The warm, moist conditions encouraged an insect paradise and the cubs scratched continually, irritated by the fleas. This invited long hours during the middle of the day for de-fleaing.

With the rain, the frog population exploded, turning the nights into multi-layered concerts of song, ranging from the deep sonorous dirge of the bullfrogs to the liquid call of the tree frog. Little Boy kept cool during the day flopped at the edge of his favourite pond, a furrow of trapped rainwater at the side of the donga floor. Soon the cubs were chasing after the frogs as they leapt around the edges of the pools. When they caught their first frog, they neither bit it nor extended their claws into its flesh. While it scrabbled around, both of them rolled sideways and forwards over their shoulders in glee, shooting out a paw periodically to flatten the frog to the ground each time it jumped. The cubs were more curious about learning the physical properties of the frog than trying to kill it and eat it: that it jumps but can't jump when pinned to the ground; that its eyes bulge when it is squashed; that it pops back into shape after being flattened. Eventually, the frog staggered off under a bush and the cubs lost interest.

They spent many happy hours chasing lizards and skinks with frenzied little fox hops through the grass. They left several tailless escapees making off into the undergrowth – the number of disembodied tails left lying on the sandy floor of the donga mounted daily.

Characteristic of a lowveld summer, the thunderclouds rolled in in the early afternoon. The low, growling noise and the violent claps of thunder didn't alarm the cubs. They simply stared skywards and wrinkled their noses slightly.

There was a curious contradiction in the cubs' nature. While we improvised new games constantly to challenge their love of novelty, they resisted change. For filming, JV, Elmon and I wore the same style of clothes, buying three or four sets of shirts and shorts to assist with the continuity of filming and to make the editing easier in post-production. The others in the team kept to the dress code of the bush – khaki or muted green.

One afternoon walk, it started raining. Karin pulled a blue plastic raincoat from her backpack and put it on for the first time.

Little Girl became apprehensive, walking a distance from her and trying to hide. A strange expression appeared on her face and she began to behave skittishly, jumping and spinning around to confront any movement or noise. The sound of the raincoat crinkling and rubbing as Karin walked bothered her and she stalked her from a safe distance for most of the walk. Little Boy was more direct about his opinion of the weird change that had come over Karin and took a sharp slap at the raincoat around her leg, then stood back to see what would happen. Encouraged by his boldness, Little Girl jumped at her and was confused when reprimanded, responding with a guilty look and dashing off. So Karin, bighearted as always, took off the raincoat and got wet.

Graham had a similar experience when he returned from leave with an extra short haircut that nearly frightened both cubs out of their wits. Little Boy sat staring from a safe distance after dashing off, changing the angle of his head repeatedly as if hoping the image he saw would settle into a more favourable picture. After a while he allowed Graham to come nearer and stretch his hand towards him. Then, having sniffed at it, he seemed less concerned about his haircut.

The walks took on distinctly different characteristics. There were walks that were distinct patrols, when the cubs would investigate messages on the scenting posts. There were walks that were straightforward adventure expeditions, when we investigated new areas and the cubs would hunt.

Then there were routine walks where nothing obvious happened, but which were important in a more subtle way. These were the walks when Little Girl renewed her bonds with her tree friends or they were times of reminiscence, when the cubs deliberately revisited the spots that held significance for them. The russet bush willow tree of the epic Leguvaan Battle was a favourite spot. Depending on the direction the cubs chose, they would spend a few moments at the base of the tree, looking at it as if reliving this momentous event. They also hung around the film locations. Did these places hold a memory for them, not as points included in any wild leopard's patrol, but as places the cubs associated with our work together – people and leopards striving towards the common goal of recreating kinship?

Little Boy continued to regard trees as a source of fun. He never outgrew his love of bouncing on the branches and testing his weight. We were impressed by his diligence at practising this leopard skill until we realised that he was snapping the branches, savouring the sharp cracking noise they made, rather than learning whether they could sustain his weight. He expanded his repertoire of exits from the trees by turning full somersaults from the branches. When he discovered that he could right himself mid-air and land perfectly on all fours, he repeated this trick over and over again.

Little Girl regarded trees with sanctity and lay for hours in their high branches, meditating. She too came to understand the practical advantages when her brother tormented her beyond endurance. She was lighter than him and so could climb higher and escape along more slender branches. Upper reaches of trees were also a good larder for storing food away from her brother. He continued to pirate her share, pinning it to the ground with one paw while greedily stuffing back his share. He would growl at her menacingly while swallowing it all at once. His behaviour with food was more about dominance than hunger. Only in a few areas did he dominate Little Girl. In mental agility, she was streets ahead of him and not interested in proving the point.

In their respective ways, both cubs were rapidly mastering trees. Cats have a highly evolved system of balance and coordination and a complementary physiology. Their front limbs are free from attachment to the collarbone, joined by ligament and muscle, allowing free movement. Their mobile backbone enables them to twist and bend almost through 180 degrees relative to the other half of their body.

With this endowment, the cubs' acrobatics reached the sublime. There was a pattern to Little Boy's somersaulting out of the trees that looked almost choreographed, as his righting reflex kicked in. He launched himself, levelling his head first, then jackknifed his body until his face was turned to the ground. He twisted his hindquarters, using his tail to counteract his balance, then arched his back to cushion the impact of his landing. When he landed it was inevitably on all fours, his legs acting like shock absorbers. If he leapt from a high branch, he appeared to glide for a few moments like a flying squirrel, before hitting the ground.

Little Girl seldom tumbled from a tree, but ran lightly down its trunk, her paws barely touching the bark, so perfectly was her balance offset against her forward momentum. She would go up with similar grace and ease – strong hind leg energy in the leap from the ground, an agile positioning of her body with the forepaws, her tail swinging to assist with balance, culminating in an impeccable landing of great precision.

When hunting, cats possess two kinds of knowledge: their instinct, or drive, is pre-wired; the finesse of the hunt and the actual killing bite they need to learn from their mothers or through their own trial and error.

By eight months, the cubs were eager to hunt something substantial. Their pursuit of butterflies, grasshoppers, lizards, birds and frogs indicated that they had mastered a range of elementary hunting tactics. One involves a kind of stamp that leopards make on the ground immediately prior to pouncing. From a low crouched position, they take a small preliminary jump as if securing a good take-off. This creates a thumping noise thought to startle the prey and to freeze it in its tracks momentarily while they pounce. We were not quite sure how the cubs discovered this trick. Once they did, they delighted in doing it over and over again.

The cubs practised their rush by ambushing us from cover and then virtually flying at us in their enthusiasm, our severely scratched calves testifying to our role as prey. When I watched Little Girl closely, I could tell that she was assessing how well she had positioned herself, how close she had been to her target. The approach is vital, as any athlete will confirm, and Little Girl was diligently perfecting hers. After each effort she would tilt her chin slightly in a look of deep concentration, as one who is in training, debriefing herself and monitoring how well she was getting along.

During a game of soccer, Little Boy discovered a leopard hunting strategy seldom seen in the wild – launching an attack on prey from the branches of a tree. It took him the entire afternoon to master the manoeuvre. He worked out that if he hid behind the trunk of a tree and dashed out at the soccer ball, his prey, he was effectively hidden right up to the moment of his rush. Then he tried it from above and pounced from there. His improvisation was so successful that he impressed even his smart sister, who some days later copied his move. Little Boy's best efforts at ambush up until then had been to hide behind a clump of grass, too sparse to conceal him, with his bottom wriggling in the air. Now he had the tree trick as part of his repertoire, one of the most sophisticated of leopard ambushes.

Patience is the hardest thing for a predator to learn. Almost as difficult is the follow-through, which requires carefully measured timing. The tendency for the novice is to rush after the prey immediately after it has been sighted. When would the cubs try a proper hunt on an antelope, not just a chase? Our presence on the walks probably frightened off any potential prey, despite our caution. We were puzzling over a solution when the first real opportunity, discounting The Goat Rodeo in Kenya, presented itself.

The cubs' luck came in the shape of a herd of impala that moved right through the donga. This antelope, plentiful throughout most of southern Africa, is choice prey for a leopard.

With great excitement the cubs took off after the impala, sniffing at the tracks. Then, indicating that they were learning about patience, they lay upwind, well-hidden in the long grass, and waited. This type of ambush can be effective, as the herd will often wander this way and that while feeding, unaware that a predator is lying silently in wait.

Just as the herd drifted within the cubs' striking range, one snorted its alarm. The antelope defence tactic of grazing communally, each individual taking its turn to lift its head to watch for danger, had been effective. Whether the impala saw Little Boy or Little Girl hidden in the grass, or whether it was simply instinct was hard to tell. The herd took fright, swung away as one and was gone in a swirl of dust and flying hooves.

It was the nearest the cubs had ever been to impala, enabling them to note the particularity of their behaviour and the finest nuance of their movement. This contact enabled them to absorb the living scent of prey and to lock into the ancient and mystical connection between predator and prey, for the cubs now but one step from consummation.

There were similar situations in the next few weeks, and just when it seemed that the task was too difficult for the cubs, nature, in her overarching way, tipped the odds.

Late in the afternoon on a walk north of the camp, Little Girl suddenly became purposeful about her movement, focusing ahead with intent. None of us heard or saw anything as she slunk off into a thicket in a stalk. Taking our cue from her, we all dropped into a crouch and kept still. From up ahead came a crying noise, and we moved forward to see Little Girl with her front paw pinning a duiker fawn to the ground. She was uncertain about exactly where to bite. That moment of hesitation proved to be her undoing.

The mother duiker came charging at Little Girl, scaring her just enough to release her hold slightly. In that moment, the duiker fawn escaped. Little Girl was out of steam. She hung back as the duiker family fled. It was a sign of an unusually mature analytic ability to assess her chances so decisively and not to waste further energy. For the rest of that day adrenalin surged through Little Girl and she was alert and responsive to every sound or movement. She had perfected the pounce and catch part of her hunt. Next time she could work out the actual killing bite technique.

Antelope hunting dominated our walks after that incident, exhausting and challenging us to find ways of getting the cubs back to camp in their adrenalin-pumped state.

The cubs were developing better judgement. Once, deep in the woodland, a lion called. I was nervous, thinking it was nearby, but the cubs showed no undue alarm. They paused, cocked their heads, swivelled their ears and then continued, clearly satisfied that our range was safe from the lion. As with all cats, a leopard's hearing is a super-sense. They can hear over two octaves higher than we can. Being able to discriminate finely between different tones in a sound, they can pinpoint its source.

When hunting expeditions took us into unfamiliar areas, the cubs displayed an uncanny homing instinct. Cats have some kind of perception that science cannot account for at present. No matter where they were in the bush, in the absence of familiar landmarks and in all types of weather, they would head for home. It was as if they were guided by energy frequencies.

At a year old, the cubs were becoming enormously powerful. They displayed spectacular leaps after the soccer ball, rubber thong and frisbee. Little Boy once achieved an impressive two-and-a-half-metre jump from a sitting position. With a run-up, he managed almost four metres. His physique was maturing more quickly than his sister's, with a growing depth to his chest muscles.

Little Girl remained slight in build, yet advancing mentally in leaps and bounds. She revealed a lightning-quick mind and a rare capacity to analyse and foresee events, and to pre-empt trouble.

While growing up, Little Boy continued to amuse us unintentionally. Early one morning his voice began to break, giving his calls the depth and volume of an adult male. At first he didn't get the tempo of the call right, and there was an odd tremolo piece in the middle of the normal rasping.

Both cubs developed that characteristic walk of big cats – a supple, loose-wristed flicking action of the front paws.

The baboons that moved through the area remained a source of terror to the cubs. They raided T'Ingwe camp, repeatedly hurling themselves noisily up and down nearby trees, ripping branches and yelling from the safety of the branches in a show of strength. It is a common fallacy that leopards' favourite prey is baboon. A well-experienced leopard hunter will prey on a baboon, but an adult male baboon is so powerful he could rip a leopard cub apart with his hands. The males work cooperatively and a group of them banding together against a predator in defence of their youngsters can prove to be an intimidating army.

The look of disgust on Little Girl's face suggested that the baboons' language had offended her. The vocal assault of a troop is so coarse and discordant in comparison to the refinement of leopard communication, which is vocally basic. The rest of their communication is through subtle yet eloquent body talk, or gently travels in other dimensions, from mind to mind.

We were becoming a team. The cubs enabled us to avoid any unexpected confrontation in the bush. If any less brazen visitor than the baboons passed by T'Ingwe camp on its night patrol, the cubs always alerted us to its presence. They showed reluctance to come out of the boma in the morning, the pupils of their eyes dilated and their body talk indicating their hesitance. Inevitably, we would later pick up tracks of a lion or hyena that had passed close by. To confirm their story, the cubs showed us on the walk that intruders had moved through the area by sniffing persistently at the bases of trees and bushes for scent messages.

Each new scent held intrigue, and if there was nothing fresh the older trails were as exciting the second or third time around. They sniffed at a scent quite noisily and then analysed it via the vomeronasal organ. This organ feeds the chemical scent message to two receptor sites; to that part of the brain responsible for sensory perception as well as to the limbic system, which triggers emotional or sexual response. To push the odour molecule to this organ, also known as 'the organ of Jacobson', they open the mouth, wrinkle the nose and curl up the tongue. They look incredibly stupid as they stand 'flehming' with half a snarl, half a smile and a puzzled expression in their eyes. This rates as one of the most undignified, and funniest, expressions I have ever seen on a cat's face.

With all the flehming, we should have interpreted the signs. The second clue came when Little Girl, some distance ahead of her brother, waited in ambush for him. He was sniffing intently at the leaves of a gwarrie bush, trying to analyse a chemical message, when he looked up. He failed to recognise the leopard he saw as being his sister and responded fearfully by raising his head and swaying it from side to side repeatedly, his ears flattened. He wouldn't approach Little Girl at first but made repeated harsh puffing noises, until she reassured him with her own gentler puffing greeting that it was indeed her.

Little Girl also displayed inappropriately fearful behaviour, on occasions stubbornly refusing to return to camp. Once she hid down a warthog hole. At other times she stayed up trees, despite her favourite toys being dangled in front of her. We put this down to her temperamental moods.

One day, after she had irritated everyone by sitting out for hours in the heat, we left her in the boma and Little Boy went out for a game of soccer on his own in the donga below the camp. Little Boy had become a real soccer star with a wide range of leaps and swats, but with a major drawback. Each time he captured the ball, his need for possession and dominance emerged and he bit into it hard, adding yet another casualty to the growing number of 'dead' soccer balls in the camp.

It was an odd day. With hindsight and more sensitivity perhaps, we might have seen a thread running through the clues around us. The moon was in Aries – a dangerous aspect for Little Boy. Did he know when he awoke that day that it was going to be one of some significance? He had a feeling of invincibility about him, seen in the excessive bounce in his legs. It was that combination of pride, boldness and overconfidence, which humans call hubris. Little Girl watched her brother that morning and noted the swagger in his step with apprehension. Little Boy was on the prowl. She had seen her brother that way before and knew that nothing could influence him. Ordinarily she might have encouraged him to somersault out of the bush willow tree, but a prickly sensation somewhere at the back of her head made her uncomfortable. She was aware of unusual signals in her mind and sensed strange messages coming from the earth. She spent most of her day up a broad-boughed mopani tree and later, hiding down a hole that she'd found. How were either of the cubs to foresee what would happen that afternoon? Little Boy was heading for a fall, and Little Girl had a premonition of what was to come.

As he walked down into the donga that afternoon to play soccer, Little Boy killed the remaining pieces of Leppie savagely. If he had been more circumspect by nature, he might have recognised that this recklessness was clouding his perspective.

First, there was a gunshot. I heard the high revving of a Landrover engine. Karin's. There was trouble. No one drove at that speed in the bush unless there was an emergency. When I heard Karin shouting for help, I felt a sickening sensation in the pit of my stomach. I was beside her in the Landrover before the vehicle drew to a halt. Elmon wasn't far behind. He had also heard the commotion.

We reversed from the parking space and swerved off at such a pace that Elmon and I almost flew out of our seats. As we drove, Karin blurted out the story.

'Little Boy's been attacked … quickly … a wild leopard … he's gone!' She was almost incoherent with shock, trying to catch her breath.

Elmon barely speaks English, but his non-verbal skills are sharp. From behind me I heard the cold click of metal as he loaded his rifle. Within seconds we circled back to T'Ingwe camp, broadsided to a halt and leapt from the vehicle, dashing for the track that led from the tents. We crashed through the long, tangled grass and reeds. We were all desperately searching for tracks.

Not far ahead, to our astonishment, we saw Little Boy washing in the sun, ignoring us completely. We drew up to a jumbled halt and stared at him and then at each other. We talked all at once, moving towards Little Boy and cooing reassurances and relief at seeing him. Little Boy continued to wash studiously, the way cats do when they want to pretend that everything is under control.

The quickened beating of his heart and the slightly furtive shift of his eyes revealed another message. He stood up, stretched casually, then strolled back towards camp and nonchalantly lay down in the shade. He stared at his rescue party with the steadiest of gazes, as if we were insane. We stood there armed to the teeth, a group of desperados brandishing rifles and sticks.

I wasn't surprised by his cover-up when I learnt that it was Little Boy who had initiated the aggression. He always tended to be bolshy under the current aspect of Aries. Apparently, our hero had been knocking the soccer ball around alongside his boma when suddenly he flattened his ears, stared fixedly down the donga, puffed a few times and then charged off on a mission. Without warning, he dropped to the ground as if stalking something, slunk through the bushes and vanished into the curve of a river bed.

It was then that Karin had lost sight of him. After a period of silence, furious hissing and spitting erupted from the reed bed. A blur of spotted fur streaked past, followed closely by another flash of fur and fury. Karin drew her handgun and shot a warning into the air to chase off what she realised with horror was a wild leopard fighting with Little Boy. A moment of silence followed the retort, then grunting and snarling began building up in the reeds.

She raced back to the camp, banging on the food cupboard door, smacking the food bowl loudly against the table and the cub grub container, in desperation going through the whole repertoire of food calls to lure Little Boy from his crazy battle with the wild leopard. Then, fearing Little Boy might be killed, she jumped into the Landrover to fetch us, choosing to drive rather than run so she could call for help on the vehicle's radio.

Elmon picked up two sets of tracks in the donga. We walked up and down, reading the story that the earth had to tell us. The foreign tracks appeared to be those of a young female leopard. There had been a vigorous skirmish, judging by the swirls in the sand and the litter of broken vegetation lying scattered through the reed bed. Little Boy emerged from the incident without any visible injury, apart from losing several clumps of fur. None of us of would ever really know exactly what had happened between the two leopards.

After the Incident with the Wild Leopard, we were assured that Little Boy was not short on courage, although I felt he might be lacking in common sense.

For the next few weeks, Little Boy led the walk. He chose to walk in the opposite direction to where The Incident had taken place, suggesting that it hadn't been all plain sailing for him. The day following The Incident, he began marking territory for the first time. He urinated backwards on tufts of grass with gusto. He would back up, holding his tail vertically and vibrating it with intensity, while he trod the ground repeatedly as he sprayed. After releasing the fluid, he would kick a shower of sand up backwards with a flourish, as if he were putting an exclamation mark to the message he was writing on the bush.

We memorised the track of the wild leopard and began to recognise fresh tracks frequently in and around T'Ingwe camp. After cross-checking our findings with the lodge, we heard that a ranger had located a young female leopard in our vicinity and identified her as the granddaughter of Mother Leopard, the daughter of the Tugwaan female. From the records kept of the leopards of Londolozi, this young female would be ready for mating. She had most likely been pushed sideways from her mother's home range, as female leopards often are, and was looking to occupy a neighbouring territory.

Her bold behaviour suggested that she might well be in oestrus. Perhaps she fancied Little Boy and the encounter in the donga was not an aggressive territorial confrontation, but rather a case of Little Boy having misread her seductive intentions.

The young female leopard returned to the camp a second time. We heard a massive scrap going on in the boma with an unusually vicious tone to it, different from the usual spat between Little Boy and Little Girl. As Graham approached the boma, a wild leopard flew past him and stood brazenly on a log at the edge of the clearing, glaring at the cubs. Both of them were securely inside the boma at the time so there was no contact, but Little Girl was shocked and pacing and Little Boy was breathless with fear. No heroism this time.

The third time Tugwaan's daughter visited, she again stood boldly one night at the end of the camp next to Andries' tent, hardly fazed when he shone a flashlight at her. She dropped down into the grass, but didn't run away, leaving us puzzled by her brashness. The following morning the vervet monkeys' alarm indicated that she was still around the camp.

Whatever passed between the wild leopard and Little Boy had a lasting effect on him. He marked territory, spraying every bush in sight around the camp. He was thoroughly confused by the whole episode. At night we heard him make strange, sawing, coughing sounds, in the way mature leopards call to each other. Perhaps his hormones were responding after all. Technically, Little Boy would be ready for mating in only two years' time, but the lessons of etiquette surrounding the process appeared to have come Little Boy's way early on.

The Incident with the Wild Leopard was a harsh reminder that our time with the cubs was limited and that we needed to gear our minds to our inevitable separation and their release into the wild.

Leopard mothers disperse their cubs when they are anything from nine months to two years old. With Little Boy and Little Girl, we knew one of two things might happen. Because of our inadequacy as human guardians, either they would become independent at a younger age, drawing from deep within themselves, or they would take longer to learn what they needed to know. Either way, we needed to be as ready as we could, both emotionally and logistically. We were unable to release the cubs at Londolozi, as the game reserve is a wildlife tourist destination with a large human settlement in the neighbouring villages. Because the cubs were hand-raised, we needed to find them a home in a more remote part of Africa, far away from any human habitation.

Such areas are hard to find, as 'wild Africa' is a romantic notion, reminiscent of a past long-gone. Human populations have spread right across the continent. Shortly after the feature film shoot, JV went on a recce, searching through southern Africa for a home for the leopards. In Zambia, the wildlife authorities agreed to allow us to complete our work by releasing the cubs in a remote area of the South Luangwa National Park, a vast wildlife area.

Before we could leave for Zambia, one of the most critical scenes in the movie still needed to be shot. It had been delayed because of a hold-up in making a dummy crocodile. It was a difficult scene to shoot, as it required Little Boy and Little Girl to be on camera for the duration of the action, with no human actors to help carry it along. The scene was pivotal to the story and it was vital that it was dramatic and credible.

In the scene, JV is in Kenya persuading the Maasai elders to allow him to release the cubs there. From the river bank, he is watching the herds of wildebeest thundering across the Mara River in their annual mass migration. One and a half million wildebeest and zebra moving in a swathe across east Africa, from Tanzania to Kenya and back, following the rains and the abundant grazing.

As JV is watching this spectacle, he is distracted from keeping an eye on the cubs. Little Boy slips down to the edge of the river to get a closer look. An enormous crocodile lies in ambush, as they have done for thousands of years to hunt the migrating animals. From beneath the surface of the murky water, the crocodile torpedoes out of the water, snatches Little Boy in its jaws and drags him into the water to his death.

The scene in our film captures the efficiency of this ruthless predator in action. It is a heart-wrenching moment; coming after the audience has taken the brave little leopards into their hearts. They have lived with the cubs through their struggle to survive. Then, just as they are poised to re-enter the wilderness, Little Boy is killed.

We planned to shoot this part of the Kenyan sequence at a dam at Londolozi. The sequence was filmed with a series of dummy crocodiles and dummy leopards, but we did hope to film the cubs in the scene as fully as we could, their reactions giving the moment a deeper emotional charge. To shoot the scene was a logistical Everest. We had two model crocs, one of them with a moveable lower jaw for the close-up shot of it clamping down fatally on Little Boy. A technician standing off-camera operated a range of levers in the back of its head. The other dummy was the full body of the crocodile, concealed in wait under the water, attached by wires to a winch on a vehicle parked on the shore.

The idea was to get Little Boy to the edge of the water, lured by the reward of a scrub hare dangling from a wire strung overhead. Then, as he moved towards the water's edge, the apparatus would launch into action. The dummy croc would leap out of the water. Little Boy would stare in horror, facing certain death. Then, cut to a close-up of the other model croc crushing the dummy leopard in its jaws. The next shot would be of Little Girl calling plaintively from the shore as she sees her brother in the jaws of death. Finally, JV was to leap into the water, stabbing at the escaping croc with his Maasai spear in a futile attempt to save Little Boy.

Both cubs were suspicious right from the early morning of the day scheduled to film, sensing something untoward when we tried to load them into the vehicle. They were completely attuned to any heightened tension around them. Little Girl resisted so staunchly that she was left behind in T'Ingwe camp for the morning. Little Boy was driven alone in his travelling box to the edge of the dam. He was alert the moment he emerged from the box and even when his attention was drawn to the meat dangling from a wire at the water's edge, he hesitated – unusual for Little Boy. The temptation of the snack gradually got the better of him and he edged cautiously towards the water.

Then, with a shock of horror, he saw the dummy croc half-submerged in the water. He hissed and spat, spun around and scrambled for the cover of a pile of boulders lying some metres away, which wouldn't budge. No matter how much he wanted that scrub hare, his instincts told him that he was in grave peril, despite never having seen a crocodile before. The crew tried all sorts of tricks to confuse him, even concealing the croc under hessian cloth. Even though he seemed less reactive when he couldn't see the croc, he wasn't entirely fooled and snuck around looking way too

*Above:* Leopard silhouettes against the African sunset.
*Below:* The cubs play in a thorn tree against a vermilion sky.

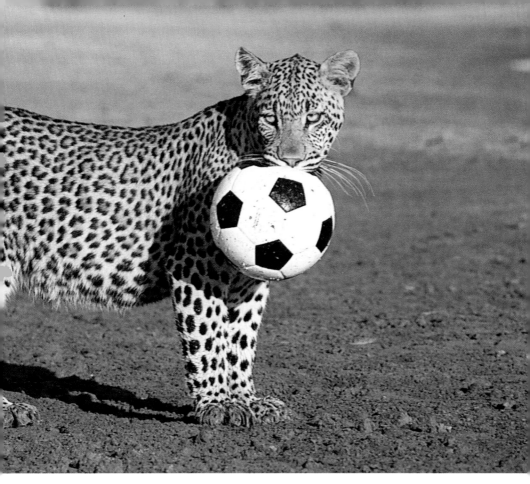

*Top left: The back of Little Boy's head shows perfect symmetry. The white tips on leopard's ears are thought to act as following mechanisms.*
*Left: JV and Little Boy cool off during a soccer game on a sandbank in Zambia.*
*Above: Little Boy's idea of soccer was total possession of the ball.*
*Right: Little Boy's attempt to ambush Jackson at the water cart is foiled.*

*Above:* Preparation for the pounce is everything.
*Below:* Little Boy hoists a carcass into a tree to prevent piracy from hyenas.
*Right:* The Great Leguvaan Battle.

*Where angels fear to tread – Little Boy rushes in to hunt a porcupine, ending up with several quills stuck through his paw.*

**Above:** *Little Boy soon realised that guinea fowl were easier prey.*
**Left:** *Little Boy's first encounter with a python.*

*Right:* A Maasai warrior tentatively greets
Little Boy.
*Below:* The Maasai and their cattle prepare
for the film shoot.

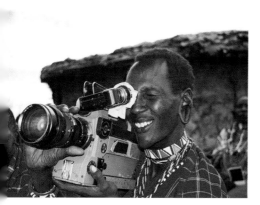

*Far left:* Nomajoli, one of our Maasai friends, in her fine beads.
*Top:* Lekuken, a Maasai elder, tries his hand at rolling film.
*Centre:* Little Boy in the wide open grasslands of Kenya.
*Below:* Brooke Shields gets to know Little Boy at Londolozi.

**Top left:** Brooke, JV and Little Boy pose for publicity shots.
**Left:** Preparing to photograph the cubs.
**Below:** Little Boy's reaction to seeing himself on 'screen'.

*Top:* Brooke and JV on the film set of
Running Wild.
*Centre:* Shooting the dramatic crocodile
scene.
*Bottom:* Karin and I with Little Boy in the
donga at Londolozi.

*The magnificence of a fully grown African leopard.*

*Above:* Preparing to cross over – Little Girl watches in horror as her brother enters the water.
*Left:* Little Boy is determined to leave.
*Below:* Little Boy swims away from T'Ingwe camp – his first move to independence.

furtive to give a convincing performance. We had to pack up and post-pone shooting the scene until later.

That afternoon, we managed to take Little Girl along as well. She hadn't seen the dummy croc and didn't know there was danger in the water. The crew had taken the precaution of concealing the dummy under hessian cloth. Little Boy, with his memory of the morning's terror, hung back behind the boulders and encouraged his sister to do the same. Then, see-ing his little sister about to get the scrub hare, he found courage and crept tentatively alongside Little Girl, taking a long route around through whatever cover he could find.

At that critical moment, the technical crew sprang into action, activat-ing the winch. The croc lunged from the water but the apparatus was sluggish in comparison to the lightning reactions of the cubs. By the time the dummy croc made its dramatic lunge, the cubs had scattered into the bulrush thickets at the edge of the dam. The scene was a disaster.

The shoot degenerated into farce as we improvised ways of capturing the action. Technicians waded around in the water, manually snapping the dummy croc's jaws at the dummy leopard. There was lots of splash-ing, shouting and hysteria. In the end Duncan, weak with laughter, called it a wrap, figuring he could make the scene work with some clever cut-ting on the editing table.

While chaos reigned on set, I sat on the bank, keeping an eye on the cubs who were still shell-shocked and hiding in the shrubs. The scene was nearly in the can and while Duncan was working on the close-up shots, the croc dummy was dragged out of the water and left to dry on the bank. After a while, Little Boy poked his head from out of the shrubs and began to move stealthily around the gardenia bush. I thought he was going to panic as he was confronted unexpectedly by the croc when he rounded the shrub.

But he appeared to be making his way intentionally towards the dummy croc, carefully under cover of the thorn bushes and the rocks. Then, with a little run, he slunk up next to the gardenia bush. Dropping into a magnificent crouch, he waited patiently. Sensing the croc had not spotted him, he pounced onto the croc's back and bit it hard on the head.

The rubber tore and to Little Boy's surprise, a large chunk came off in his mouth as the force of his leap spun him flat on his back with a thud. He lay winded alongside the monster, with a chunk of the croc's head dangling from the side of his mouth. He spat out the rubber and laid into the croc with a volley of smacks from his front paws, his ears pulled sharply backwards. Facing the crocodile from so close must have unnerved him, for his courage failed. He turned tail and fled back to where Little Girl was hiding in the bush, peeping anxiously from behind a branch.

Tears of laughter and surprise rolled down my cheeks and a wave of tenderness welled up inside me. At the same time, I hoped the cubs retained scary memories of the dangers posed by water and crocodiles. We were destined for the Luangwa Valley in Zambia. The Luangwa River, which runs down the centre of the valley, has a density of crocodiles higher than any other body of water in Africa.

As I sat there at the side of the dam, I felt a chill of apprehension. This episode with the croc showed how young and inexperienced the cubs really were. Were they ready for a life of independence? We had exposed them to the challenges and potential dangers of the wilderness; crocodiles, snakes, lions, the demands and territorial imperatives of other leopards and the rivalry of predators. We had nurtured an appropriate sense of wariness and encouraged them to hunt, protecting them when they made mistakes and went after warthogs or giraffe, prey far too large and dangerous for them.

Little Girl, so adept in the trees and so talented a hunter, was so fragile and gentle a spirit. Little Boy, though impressively muscular in his chest, was still round in his tummy and foolishly brave in his heart. Were they ready to take on freedom?

# CHAPTER SIX

# *Siya ekhaya*

*We are going home*

Once again, Little Boy and Little Girl lay at the rear of an aircraft, their lives accelerating through time and space. It was as though they were spiralling through a wormhole linking two dimensions. When they awoke from the immobilising drugs, they would be in their new home in the South Luangwa National Park in Zambia. Here they would face the transition to becoming wild leopards.

If true wilderness exists in the Africa of today, it is here in the Luangwa National Park, 14 000 km² of habitat so inhospitable that nature has preserved herself in a virtually pristine state. For a large part of the year temperatures rise upwards of 40 °C with humidity reaching saturation point. Torrential rain of the summer months makes access to the interior of the region impossible. More hazardous than this climate are nature's own warriors, the anopheles mosquito bearing fatal strains of malaria, and the tsetse fly. Limited ecotourism does exist in the brief winter months, utilising a small section of the park, the bulk of it remaining a barely explored wilderness. In this untouched Eden, the wild species of Nature's kingdom thrive in a diversity of plant, animal and bird life. Because of its seclusion, this is also prime leopard habitat.

The southern boundary of the Park is the Luangwa River, a tributary of the Zambezi, one of the great rivers of Africa. It winds along the floor of a sharply incised valley forming the southwesterly extent of the Great Rift Valley, the vast continental fault which clefts vertically through Africa from the Red Sea in the north. It is a volatile river, the Luangwa, the turbulent floodwaters of the wet season receding into streams winding amiably through the flood plains during the dry months. Some kilometres downstream from the small town of Mfuwe not far from Zambia's eastern border with Malawi, a small island lies in the river. This was to be our new home – T'Ingwe Island.

The Cessna swung southeast from Lusaka, following the length of the valley to Mfuwe Airport. We flew at a fairly low altitude, the landscape so vast and wide beneath us that I imagined I could see the curvature of the earth.

The drone of the aeroplane brought a discordant note to this lost Eden, momentarily disturbing the wild inhabitants of the valley. In the slipstream of noise, flocks of white cattle egrets rose from their perch and swirled like drifts of snow against the clear blue sky. Herds of zebra looked up from grazing, wheeled and galloped across the flood plains, the white and black stripes of their coats stark against the sandy flood plains of the river bed. Along the banks, large groups of pink-bellied hippos rose heavily to their feet from their snooze and trundled to the safety of their pools. Startled by the collective commotion around them, herds of puku took flight, dancing through the shallows at the water's edge, sending a rainbow spray of water glistening from their hooves.

The wilderness of the South Luangwa Park stretched endlessly, a mosaic of texture and colour. At the edge of the river, the flood plains were flushed with the lime green sheen of new grass. Alongside ran a stain of dark green forested vegetation. Moving towards the escarpment, the habitat stretched into mopani woodlands criss-crossed with a network of winding paths, trodden by the thousands of hooves travelling through the forests to and from drinking places and grazing areas. Beyond the flood plains, the river curved and meandered, forming lagoons and oxbow lakes in and around the loads of silt. This silt was deposited during the rainy season when the river, swollen with floodwater, raged in a torrent down the valley, scouring its banks, uprooting trees and bearing the debris down along its course.

It was a journey of five or six hours from Londolozi to our new home. The flight had been interrupted by refuelling stops and red tape at the airports. We were up before daybreak that morning, moving like shadows around the camp, our mood solemn, in deference to this rite of passage facing Little Boy and Little Girl. There was a sublimated excitement amongst us at the prospect of what lay ahead in Zambia, but that would find expression later. The task of relocating the cubs was serious business.

Because of the stress of such a long and noisy flight with its anticipated interruptions, we chose to sedate Little Boy and Little Girl. Dewalt Keet, the state veterinarian from the neighbouring Kruger National Park, was to accompany us and monitor their progress. To distract the cubs from our devious intentions, we staked a warthog carcass in their boma, hoping that, while they were feeding, Dewalt could get a clear shot with the dart gun.

Once again, we underestimated Little Girl's sensitivity to nuance and atmosphere. She was suspicious and nervous from the moment activity began in the camp that morning, watchful of our every move from the shadows at the rear of the boma. She held back from the meat, even though she was hungry. The sounds of her brother feasting with abandon drew her forward tentatively.

Dewalt managed to get an accurate shot into her upper hind leg, but as the dart hit, she barked with shock and pain, alerting Little Boy to the danger. He stared at her in surprise as she reeled from the impact and watched incredulously as the red-feathered tail of the dart fell from her thigh. Both of them hissed and spat viciously at Dewalt, who had tried to conceal himself so that the cubs would not imprint a negative association of humans hurting them. I felt that the worse the association the cubs made in their memories of a human carrying a gun, the better for them. Hunters and poachers were a reality in the landscape of their future.

It was a long time before we could distract Little Boy from his suspicion of foul play, especially when his sister began to stagger and fall in front of him. Finally, they both lay outstretched and unconscious on the tarpaulin, with their pink tongues hanging from the sides of their mouths. Little Girl looked so vulnerable, as did Little Boy now that all the energy expressed in his vigorous movement was stilled.

For one horrible moment we nearly lost Little Girl when her heartbeat faltered. The drug dosage is based on an estimation of weight and this, combined with individual reaction, can be unpredictable. Little Girl's heart rate fell suddenly.

Dewalt sprang into action. Although he worked calmly, his movements certain and unrushed, I could read anxiety in his eyes and the beads of sweat on his forehead. He managed to stabilise her condition. I felt almost winded by the shock and the suddenness with which fate could have changed everything and yet relieved that we'd handed over this part of the relocation work to Dewalt, such a competent and experienced vet.

The cubs were laid on a mattress in the back of the Landrover. The sky was grey and overcast, unusual for early autumn. A light drizzle began to fall and, while rain is a blessing in the bush, that day it added to the gloominess of the atmosphere.

This was the beginning of goodbye. We had mixed feelings as the aeroplane took off and we watched Londolozi recede: hope for the cubs who were leaving their cubhood behind; apprehension for the realities their future life held; sad for us, as this relocation meant moving closer to the time that Little Boy and Little Girl would leave us. We would return to Londolozi, but there would be no going back for the cubs.

The pilot veered the Cessna slightly away from our course along the Luangwa River and approached for landing at Mfuwe Airport. From above we could see the local people leaving their thatched mud huts, making their way to the airfield. The story of Little Boy and Little Girl's arrival had preceded us. Although they lived in such close proximity to one of the greatest wilderness areas in Africa, most villagers would never have seen a leopard, creatures so secretive by nature and so aware that their safety lay in seclusion, beyond the reach of people. We waited on the airstrip and, while the customs officials went through the paperwork, swung open the door of the aeroplane to allow fresh air to flow through. The warm, damp heat outside hit us like a wall. The villagers, now in their hundreds, gathered around the aeroplane door laughing and chatting loudly in wonder at the spectacle before them.

They were gentle-eyed people, the folk from Mfuwe village, with wide smiles and a cheerful music in their language. They shoved eagerly around the door, necks craning, pressing forward, while sheltering themselves from the heat of the sun with brightly coloured umbrellas. They were curious to see the cubs, but more than that, they wanted to touch them. I knew it went beyond the rarity of the opportunity and the sensuality of stroking such beautifully rosetted fur. In that momentary connection, they came into contact with something so utterly wild, they reconnected with a part of themselves long forgotten.

The second stage of the relocation required a helicopter, as our camp on T'Ingwe Island was a few kilometres further downstream and difficult to access. Space inside the chopper was limited and with Rob, the pilot, JV, Dewalt and the cubs on board, there was no room for Karin and I. We made the journey by road, planning an overnight stop at Tundwe Lodge outside Mfuwe and completing the journey to T'Ingwe Island the following day by bushtrail and boat. It was distressing to be separated from the cubs at this delicate stage. When Dewalt gave them the antidote, they would be safe in their temporary cages. They would have each other for support and the privacy and solitude that cats need in which to recover their strength and regain their control and sense of equilibrium.

As it turned out, Karin and I should have been more concerned about our own journey from Mfuwe than about the cubs. We drove with our friends the Patels, who own Tundwe Lodge, down a bush track eroded by heavy rain. Progress was slow, even in the robust four-wheel drive. The recent downpour had left the deeply rutted roads coated with a thick layer of slippery mud and wide stretches of water.

The way I was taught to handle such seemingly impassable roads was to engage low-range gears and diff-lock and, while keeping the revs of the engine up, to maintain a sure and steady pace until out of trouble. Clearly they did things differently in Zambia. With a whoop from Gulam, more like a war cry, the vehicle lurched forward. We accelerated wildly, going full tilt at one of the large puddles. The vehicle hit the mud and spun around a full 360 degrees. I thought in that moment we were going to flip over. Round and round we spun, with Gulam roaring with laughter, an infectious, deep and resonant kind. The vehicle came to a skidding halt broadside on and we disentangled ourselves from one another.

'Now you see why we can't get eggs to the camp!' he boomed.

After a few more similar episodes, we arrived at Tundwe Lodge just after dark, bruised, shaky and splattered with mud.

Rob, JV and Dewalt had already returned in the chopper.
'The cubs are fine,' Dewalt reassured us. 'In better shape than you!'

It was a shock to see them the next day. They looked dishevelled, with their fur lacklustre and matted. Little Girl looked frail, her eyes hollow and her expression strained. Even Little Boy, with his usually buoyant temperament, looked sorry for himself and cried pitifully when he saw us. Both of them jumped visibly at the slightest movement or noise. The drugs had left them with headaches and they were physically uncoordinated. The cubs were clearly overwhelmed. Nothing they perceived around them was familiar, not the sounds, the smells, the energies. Nothing their senses reported to them was familiar. For a wild animal, especially a cat, this incapacity and loss of control is devastating, for it makes them feel psychologically exposed and vulnerable.

The cubs' favourite toys were with them in their cage, the string mop, the impala tail on the string and even the pathetic remains of Leppie and Lion. Even these old faithfuls were unable to reassure them. It was the same as when they had left their birth mother. I hoped that some memory of their survival then would help them through this experience.

It took a long time for the cubs to work through the effects of the drugs. Little Boy and Little Girl seemed depressed. They responded to us by being overly affectionate in a way we had never known. We took turns to sit with them. When I sat in the boma that morning, both cubs lay against me or on my body, drawing warmth and reassurance. I was distressed to see them regressing to cubhood dependence, even if it was temporary. Little Girl cowered with every sharp movement and both cubs began pacing within their new boma.

One option was to leave them be, for that is the choice for a wild leopard struggling with injury or stress. Clearly though, Little Boy and Little

Girl were reaching out to us. I did bodywork with them and some of their jitteriness subsided as the blocked energy of fear was released. We needed a mechanism to draw their attention away from their wider disorientation and bring it into present time. It was sad to see even Little Boy turn away from his beloved food bowl.

Then Karin tumbled onto an unusual distraction while sorting out boxes and baggage at the camp. She unpacked a container of fabric softener and saw a use for it immediately. She remembered Little Girl's fascination with its scent and so made a few impromptu toys from socks and clothes, dipped them into the liquid and tied them on a string as lures. What a joyful find. Soon the cubs were fighting for possession. Though wobbly on their paws with muscles bruised and inflamed from the injections, there was an instant change. The vacant expression in their eyes gave way to one of lively interest.

We wanted to re-establish ritual in the cubs' daily experience – to find a new rhythm and a structure, to orientate them in their new habitat, to begin the daily sunrise and sunset walks so they could piece together the environmental puzzle around them. There was work to be done. There were new routes to set up, new landmarks to identify, new scents to discover, new play areas to establish, new reconnaissance points to be worked out and new scenting posts to be created. The cubs needed to map the area. All potential threats or hazards within their new home range had to be assessed, ambush spots set up and, most important of all, relationships needed to be sorted out with the other inhabitants of the area. The cubs had to feel some control over their lives and this was the only certain way.

It took a few days before the cubs felt well enough to do anything adventurous. On the first walk, Little Boy bravely took the lead, with Little Girl following nervously at his shoulder. They slunk out of the boma, their bodies low to the ground, their ears swivelling. Some few metres from the boma, Little Boy lost his nerve and bolted back into the cage. After a short while, he regained his courage and then tried again.

Once out of camp, Little Girl tried to jump on a fallen tree, but the drugs hadn't completely worn off. Her ability to retract and extend her claws had been compromised and she scrambled in vain along the log for a few paces and then fell off. Her loss of dignity was such an obvious blow to her morale and I ached for her. Her concentration and efforts were so diligent it was touching. She spent most of her time on the adventure sniffing at the base of trees, looking less I suspect for information left there than for compatible energies. New tree friends.

Little Boy fell out the first tree he climbed and, looking sheepish, stuck to the grass thickets after that. He followed a scent trail that crossed down to the sandbank at the river. The scent of water drew him down further. Perhaps memories of his adored puddle in the Inyatini Donga at Londolozi surfaced. But the vastness of this river startled him and he backed up, frightened. Was this a reminder of The Great Crocodile Attack during filming at Londolozi? For him the discovery of the river was enough exploring. For the rest of the day both the cubs kept close to camp, though joyfully there was a distinct easing of tension in their body talk after that foray.

The South Luangwa National Park lay beyond the camp, across the river to the north. That was the direction we hoped the cubs would take when they left us. JV chose T'Ingwe Island for its proximity to the park and because it was surrounded by the Luangwa River. It would remain an island for the next few months. As the waters receded in the dry season, the sandbanks in the river would join, making a land crossing to the park possible. The deeper, more permanent stream flowing on the south bank of the island would remain a barrier to the game management area, referred to as the GMA. The cubs would be protected from rival predators by the natural moat. Prey animals, including puku, impala and scrub hares would cross the sandbanks to graze on the new grasses growing on the island, giving Little Boy and Little Girl the opportunity to fine-tune their hunting skills. Then, in stages, they would enter their new life, crossing into the park.

Little Boy and Little Girl were a year old. We had no idea precisely when their independence would announce itself, when a deeper knowledge would inform them and they would go.

For us, the move to Zambia was a great adventure, the opportunity to live in one of the last wildernesses of Africa. Not so for the cubs. All the threads of meaning woven into the fabric of their lives had unravelled overnight. Yet before them, in the Luangwa National Park, lay an opportunity. If they could overcome their initial dislocation, rebuild their confidence and find within themselves whatever it took to take them across the divide, here lay the chance for them to live and to die as wild leopards.

Little Boy and Little Girl would have different challenges ahead of them. In the wild, a young male cub embarks on a journey. His mother leaves him and rejoins him periodically for protection and food. Through reading her own situation, her cub's abilities and Nature's circumstances, she guides the process of dispersal. Finally, he finds himself alone to fend for himself. As a sub-adult male, he is a potential threat to the territorial male leopard within whose home range his mother's territory lies. He will be ousted from this area and be forced to move on and on through neighbouring territories. Other dominant males will chase him in this way until he either finds an unoccupied area or until he contests and wins his own territory, unseating the male who has tenure there. If the cub survives, this rite of passage can take a couple of years.

For a young female leopard, the process is slightly gentler. Female territories are smaller, several home ranges encompassed by one territorial male. A young female leopard often has the opportunity to find a territory close to her mother's, sometimes bordering on it, even with an overlap. Leopard culture varies from area to area, depending on traditions and the demands of habitat. The social structure and rules of etiquette of the leopards in the Luangwa Valley would function slightly differently from those at Londolozi.

The Luangwa Valley offered an ideal habitat for leopards, with vast stretches of heavily bushed woodlands and forests providing cover for hunting and the seclusion so necessary to their well-being. The multitude and variety of trees, giant ebonies and mahoganies with densely branched canopies and boughs were perfect for escape, for reconnaissance, for deep sleep or to use as larders in which to cache carcasses. Dense prey populations supported large leopard numbers and territories were smaller. In many cases, several territories overlapped.

'We see a leopard on a kill, then that night, another comes. Even a third,' our Zambian game scouts, Tennis and Robert, told us. 'They don't stay to defend it, as you see at Londolozi.'

This could work to Little Boy and Little Girl's advantage. Yet the leopards of the area would be tough and robust animals, selected by the competitive culture within which they lived. Finding a niche for their own home range in this area would be a challenge.

In the meantime, we were all in it together, Little Boy, Little Girl and their support team, trying to cope on T'Ingwe Island. We empathised with the disorientation the cubs felt. Although we had planned our move from Londolozi with precision, we found ourselves thoroughly disorganised.

Our relocation plan was that when we arrived on T'Ingwe Island, the camp would be up, leaving us free to spend all our time with the cubs.

We had sent a truck on ahead, loaded with tents and provisions to see us through the first few months. We were scheduled to fly with the cubs two weeks later. The advance group, headed by John, our Zambian camp manager, would have set up camp by then. When the cubs arrived, they would move into a familiar situation, though everything beyond the camp would be strange and new. We broke camp at Londolozi in stages, packing the least essential items first, mindful of the cubs' sensitivity to any change around them, leaving their boma intact with all their toys – the string mop, the impala tail on the rope, their soccer balls in various stage of death, the frisbee and the remains of Lion and Leppie.

A combination of punctures, breakdowns and bad roads made impassable by heavy rains held up the truck. Border officials slowed their progress even further. The advance party lagged badly behind schedule, even with the cushion of time we built in for the hindrances that are an inevitable part of operating in Africa. Finally, they arrived at T'Ingwe Island just days before us. When we flew in with the cubs, the camps were not yet up.

We felt as disoriented as the cubs. Putting up the sleeping tents was one thing, but trying to produce meals for a hungry crew was entirely another. Who on earth packed several jars of cocktail olives when we couldn't find the sugar and salt? Where was the yeast, essential if we were to bake bread and how did weevils get into the flour so soon? Worse, where was the tea and coffee?

And so it went, all of us feeling frazzled and at times despondent. Only our concern for Little Boy and Little Girl and the goal of releasing them kept our focus steady and our spirits up. One look at them was all it took for me to pull myself together when weighed down by the heat or frustrated beyond endurance by camp logistics. Then, I paused and remembered what this exercise meant to them. Life or death.

Because we were working with hand-raised wild cats, our camp was far away from any of the villages in the GMA, a stretch of land that borders on national parks in the Zambian system of wildlife management. Although wild animals move freely between the two areas, the park itself is completely a wildlife preserve, while the GMA allows locals some utilisation of resources. There are hunting concessions, subsistence farming in the small villages, fishing and firewood collection. Wildlife tourism has brought some economic relief to rural poverty, with many villagers work-ing in the tourist lodges, which operate safaris near Mfuwe.

The locals from the villages were mostly Nyanja-speaking tribal people, living at the interface of human settlement and wildlife. Many families had lost children to virulent strains of malaria or crocodile attack. Others spoke of fleeing on their bicycles from elephants along the paths through the forest, or having their modest crops trampled and their food pirated.

They were a gentle people, easy-going and polite to the point of quaint-ness, diplomatic about the apparent craziness of our living with wild leop-ards. Trustingly, they accepted our word that we would protect those who came to work for us on the island. We kept Little Boy and Little Girl safe-ly in their boma while a squad of villagers helped us build the camp and kept camp numbers to an absolute minimum, as we had done at Londolozi.

Sam, a local villager, was recruited to help around the camp, doing what old Jackson had done at Londolozi, filling paraffin lamps, prepar-ing the fires and collecting wood. His wide-eyed expression and glances over his shoulder led me to suspect that, unlike his predecessor, Sam had little experience with wildlife. Two game scouts were sent from the Zambian wildlife department to monitor our project. Tennis was the older of the two men, slightly grizzled, with a conservative and dignified manner. He had worked as a migrant on the South African gold mines in his youth. Back home, he signed up as a game scout. Robert was a younger man with finely chiselled cheekbones and a smooth ebony skin. He was proud and strong and reckless, unnerving us repeatedly by plung-ing waist deep into the crocodile infested river to drag our boat free when it grounded on a sand bar. Both scouts were trained in the use of a rifle and were well informed about wildlife and the valley ecosystem. They were invaluable guides while out walking with the cubs, sharing gener-ously their insights of the complexity of the tree, plant and animal life and the legends of the valley.

Although armed and well experienced, at first they were clearly nerv-ous of the cubs. Even in their disoriented state, the cubs intimidated the two men, stalking right up close, suddenly appearing from the under-growth. Robert and Tennis soon came to understand that these tactics were more about display than serious intention. Yet, with their knowledge of the lethal capabilities of leopards, they never failed to jump when sud-denly confronted by a leopard crouching two metres in front of them.

Using their local knowledge, Robert and Tennis solved our problem of drinking water. They dug shallow wells in the sands of the flood plain alongside the river. Within hours, crystal clean river water drained into these holes, passing through Nature's own perfect sand filter. It was safer to draw water from here than to lean into the river with buckets and run the risk of confronting a tetchy hippo or a crocodile basking in the sun.

The camp was soon knocked into shape, minimal and functional. To shelter from the blazing heat, sleeping tents, the mess tent and the store tent were tucked in under the shade of the massive Natal mahogany trees with their copious foliage. To the back of the camp were the bush 'bathrooms'. The drop toilets were dug under a leafy kigelia tree and the bucket showers hung from the branches on the other side of its trunk. The ablutions were open-air facilities with surrounds for privacy. The locals cut long grass sheaths and skillfully packed them between struts and uprights made from the thinner branches of fallen mopani trees.

The showers were a simple but great joy. Hot water and soap is balm to the soul of anyone who lives and works in the hot wilderness. Showering after a hard day with stinging water heated in a fat-bellied kettle on the campfire is sheer bliss.

To the south of the camp was the mess tent, next to the dining table and chairs and the campfire. This was the centre of most camp activities. The crew ate here, held meetings, cleaned and prepared film equipment or simply sat and gazed at the beauty of Nature. The open-sided tent looked out over the vast amphitheatre of the flood plain of the river, the Luangwa Valley rising to the Muchinga Hills and the escarpment in the distance. Luxuriant riverine forest lined the banks, dominated by mahoganies, tamarinds, ebonies and kigelias, also known as 'sausage trees', bearing their distinctive heavy pods. Many of the trees were giants, testimony to the copious rainfall. Tall doon palms rose intermittently above the bushy canopy, their slender trunks and fronds an exotic silhouette against a moonlit sky, or the blazing backdrop of the setting sun. The points of the palm fronds rustled and scraped when a breeze blew, waving languidly to a music known only to them, while the tall trunk creaked and swayed. The fruit grew in clusters at the base of the fronds, each a shiny, brown nut. The Luangwa elephants were particularly fond of these fruits, stripping their leathery brown skin to eat the thin but tasty layer of flesh beneath. Often in the distance of an otherwise serene landscape, a single palm would dance and shake vigorously in a private calypso. Concealed by the lower canopy of leaves beneath, an elephant pressed its forehead against the trunk to shake the fruit loose.

We knew the cubs were recovering when they began to ambush us again. Little Boy went through his comic routine of hiding behind a tuft of grass, concealing nothing much more than his nose and eyes as he prepared to pounce. They chased each other around the tents vigorously, scaling the sides with claws screeching across the canvas before launching themselves from the tarpaulin for the 'ambush-from-above' strategy.

The cubs made a tantalizing discovery when they found laundry on a line stretched beside the kitchen tent. At Londolozi our laundry was done at the lodge, so the cubs hadn't yet experienced the joy of a shirt flapping in the breeze. The acrobatics that laundry hunting produced surpassed those of the soccer and frisbee games, although the soccer ball remained a favourite. It could be killed and collapsed audibly in defeat, hissing air noisily through its wounds. Little Boy found the ball could float and he developed a forearm strike which sent it spinning across the shallows of his new wallowing pond.

More logistical problems presented themselves. Our hunting permit from the Zambian National Parks Department went adrift and until we were authorised to shoot puku or impala in the GMA, the cubs had no food. They were not quite yet self-sustaining hunters. We bought chickens from the villagers who lived beyond Tundwe Lodge, planning to slaughter them as needed. This brought unintended comic relief to the camp. The birds kept escaping from the hutch we constructed and their constant flapping and squawking drove Little Boy and Little Girl into a frenzy. For the cubs this was clearly new prey, providing them with vicarious vengeance on the francolins that had tormented them in a similar noisy, feathery way in their early cubhood days.

Little Boy's first escaped-chicken hunt met with failure. The chicken startled him with the intensity and power of its wing beats and managed to escape. He recaptured it and began to pluck its feathers, while it squawked in outrage. Little Girl's escaped chicken went lapping off, distracting him. Little Boy lost concentration and left his catch clucking in fright in a bush and chased his sister's. On it went. We were submerged in a cloud of feathers and confusion, trying to recapture the chickens and simultaneously avoid attack by pouncing leopard cubs.

The second chicken hunt was also a near disaster. Little Boy captured one and put it in his drinking bowl, a strange habit the cubs had developed with their meat at Londolozi. This time though, his prey was still alive and the chicken, at first shocked into a state of immobility, revived instantly when it was almost drowned in the water bowl. It created such a volatile, squawking resistance that Little Boy backed off.

The cubs were really hungry and it wasn't long before they successfully killed their prey, plucked the feathers to expose the flesh and began to eat. The cubs stalked the remaining birds in the hutch relentlessly. Finally they broke in, causing pandemonium. Little Boy grabbed a chicken, bit then dropped it and went for another, as predators will do. Even when not driven by hunger, their instinct to kill is triggered by the movement of the prey in its attempt to escape. Several chickens were attacked. Some escaped, some lay dead, others fled in terror around the camp, leaving us to spend the afternoon retrieving terrified chickens from trees and bushes around the island. The following day we sent messages on the radio all day to put pressure on the authorities to issue our hunting permits.

For their first walks on T'Ingwe Island, the cubs followed the same route. As time passed they made explorative forays from the basic map as they built up their mental schemata. It was a lesson just watching this superb adaptive craft, so much a feline skill, at work.

Leopards are renowned for their ability to survive by continual adjustment to the changing environment. They have even been found living successfully close to the outskirts of cities such as Johannesburg and Nairobi. Because of this sublime ability, the leopard has the widest geographic distribution of all the large cats in the wild. Throughout the African continent south of the Sahara, eastwards across the Arabian Peninsula through Asia to Manchuria and Korea, they have adapted to dense rainforest, inhospitable desert and high mountainous regions.

As I watched this process at work I often thought of their birth mother, living in captivity in Zimbabwe. Would she feel maternal pride at the emerging skills of her offspring? How indeed would her reaction register in a leopard's range of emotions? I recalled Mother Leopard interacting with her last cub as he grew to be a fine young male, if somewhat clownish in his ways. There was no other way to describe what I read in her face, other than to call it indulgent and loving maternal pride. Would there ever be a way of describing how leopards thought and felt without projecting human emotions? Conventional scientists are sceptical of this – what they call 'anthropomorphism'.

As the days fell into a comfortable rhythm of walks, feeding, resting and playing and regular camp demolition expeditions, Little Boy and

Little Girl responded to their new home with a growing ease. In the heat and humidity a feeling of claustrophobia clung to the middle part of the day. It seemed as if during these hours nothing stirred in the valley or even breathed. The cubs spent these hours in their boma, flopped on their sides. We wove leafy branches through the wire structure, which we watered. Any slight movement of air that passed through helped to cool the cubs. We dipped our sarongs in water then wound them around our bodies. The evaporation of water gave some relief, as we lay listless in the shade. The cubs adapted much more easily than any of us, harmonising their rhythms, sleeping and waking with the demands of the habitat, often dozing or in one of their other 'sleep' modes.

Humans often dismiss sleep as the necessary rest taken between episodes of life. In a leopard's life, sleep is a vital part of living, occupying half to two thirds of a 24-hour day. In these 'sleep' hours they access complex dimensions, offering psychic enrichment as well as physical revitalisation. Wherever the cub's psyches travelled in sleep and dream work, it was visibly a busy time. In experimental work on domestic cats, EEG readings show that for 50 per cent of the 24-hour cycle, sleep is an 'active' process, a slow wave light sleep with rapid eye movements, 15 per cent is the deep sleep of restoration and the remaining 35 per cent is made up of waking hours.

When Little Boy and Little Girl were still small cubs, they slept soundly. We would scare them witless if we touched them accidentally. They would wake, snarl and spit and whip around, ready to attack. In the wild, such inobservance would make them easy prey, although at that age their mother would protect them in a den. Grown leopards climb high into the recesses of a tree and hang there lengthwise along a branch with legs dangling, their heavy and supple tail counterbalancing their weight. They relax so completely, with their head more often than not laid gently on their front paws, the flicking of their eyelids and the slightest twitching of their muscles indicating the sleep of one who is dreaming. I imagine leopards do their dream work, as humans do.

I watched the cubs as they slept, as I had often watched Mother Leopard, and wondered what form a leopard's dream work took. Apart from sifting through images and ideas, were dreams also the royal road to the unconscious, enlightening leopards through the symbolism of archetypes? Did dreamtime access universal intelligence? Did perennial wisdom flow? Reminders of individual soul choices? Contact with ancestors, perhaps?

There is so much unknowable about leopards. Hints and guesses. So much unshowable empirically but which I sensed empathetically – just as an elusive answer to a question often lingers on the tip of one's tongue, so near and yet so far from certainty. Then there were subtle intuitions, which arrived unannounced, departing as suddenly, leaving the question remaining ... 'What if?'

The classic 'catnap' is a lighter sleep state than REM – I thought the cubs were restoring their energies at a lower physical level. During this time they could instantly detect any attempt to approach them. While napping in this way, their ears would swivel like radar dishes and while their bodies were relaxed, it was with a softness that preceded action. There was the slightest thread of tension, telling of this alertness. Their reflexes in response to action were at lightning speed. What state of consciousness did this parallel in humans? Were they thinking into the past or into the future in daydreams, or were they occupying a slightly altered state of consciousness, as in meditation or prayer?

There was yet another mode of consciousness that I thought I detected as the cubs grew older. I recalled seeing this expression in Mother Leopard's eyes when we found her sitting in the branch of a tree, apparently inactive. It was a total absence of expression. Her eyes were open but vacant. It appeared as if through psychic agility, she removed her consciousness to another level away from present time, leaving the perfect skills of her physical body, her instincts and her senses to cope with the mundane tasks of the moment. In her mind she appeared to travel into dimensions unknowable. Was it a skill all leopards shared, a genetic inheritance, one that would develop as the cubs matured, or was it a more individual ability, as so many psychic talents are?

Little Boy and Little Girl were developing another mind skill – their ability to bring their consciousness perfectly into the present moment with a single focus. I saw this perfect concentration in Mother Leopard when she was hunting or in defence. Every aspect of her being was harnessed towards the task, everything else peripheral, disregarded entirely.

The stores in Mfuwe supplied basic necessities brought from the capital, Lusaka. Once a week, vendors brought vegetables to the village to a makeshift market of palm leaf stands along the one and only road that led to the airport. They sold maize, tomatoes, peanuts and cabbages, which they grew around their huts. There was no commercial farming in the area.

Market day was a colourful, sociable affair, with the women chatting loudly at their stalls, sitting on woven reed mats, legs out flat before them. And everywhere there were children. Babies slept on their mother's backs, tied there with brightly printed cloth, oblivious to the activity around them or happily feeding from the breast. Older children skipped barefoot dressed in tattered clothes, smiling shyly at strangers or chewing on raw cane sugar. More enterprising stallholders traded vegetables brought in from the larger town of Chipata on the Malawian border. Then there might be sweet oranges, avocados or paw-paws for sale.

We went to town only when we absolutely had to. The journey from T'Ingwe Island to Mfuwe began by crossing the river in our 'banana boat' – a dugout canoe. It transported fingers of bananas up and down the river. After crossing the vast sandbank in front of the camp and paddling to the opposite bank, we tied up the boat. The Landrover was parked in the shade of a tamarind tree. Then, a long, slow drive along a deeply rutted dirt track through the GMA to Mfuwe. The journey there and back took the best part of a day and often involved changing tyres, as mopani tree stumps cut into them. The return trip had to be completed before sunset. Launching the boat and landing it meant wading into the river to knee height – not a comfortable feeling even in broad daylight. The presence of crocodiles could be keenly felt. At night-time, this was practically suicidal.

Often the sole reason for the trip was to collect fuel supplies needed to run our generator and our vehicles. Fuel was available only occasionally in Mfuwe, when some entrepreneur drove a truckload of drums down from Lusaka. We stockpiled it in jerry cans when word went about that it was available.

Banana, paw-paw and mango trees surrounded many of the huts in the GMA and many of the villagers kept chickens pecking in the dirt outside their homes. The fruit and the eggs were kept mostly for family. Karin and I, both vegetarians, developed a keen eye for fresh vegetables, borne of desperation from eating the bland and anonymous tinned variety. We spotted pumpkins on the roof of a hut early on in our stay in Zambia and exchanged them for torch batteries. We became skilled at bartering. Although the trip was a saga, trading was an enjoyable way of communicating news or small talk and participating in the life of the valley.

Communication between T'Ingwe Island and the outside world was done mainly by VHF radio, but the reception was often marred by static interference. Our back-up system when the radio signal was compromised was to send Tennis or Robert on foot to the nearest game scout camp upriver or to Tundwe Lodge, in the hope that the radio there was working. If not, we could send a messenger by bicycle to Mfuwe.

All life in the valley centered on the Luangwa River. It was the dominant feature of camp life. We drew water from it, we travelled on it in our bright blue banana boat or our 'rubber duck', powered with a small motor, and we fished from the river. We spent hours simply sitting and watching it in wonder at its ever changing moods and beauty. In its gentler moments, enhanced by a golden sunset, it shone like silk, rippling as it moved. Heavy rain in the catchments brought water hurtling down the river with great crashing sounds. Cascading torrents carried uprooted trees like matchsticks in its currents. Often small creatures such as squirrels were stranded, clinging to the branches of these fallen trees and chirping in distress as they were borne downstream on their floating island. Birds sometimes chose to perch on the branches and sail downstream grandly, like figureheads of gracious ships. There was no telling what would pitch up. Sometimes dead animals would roll by on the tides; the bloated body of a dead elephant calf or a hippo with great gashes on its rump, leaving us to speculate as we sat on the bank about the story behind its death.

Beneath the waters of the Luangwa lurked more Nile crocodiles than in any other body of water in Africa; some said 14 crocodiles for every kilometre of river. Tennis and Robert warned us of a unique hunting strategy these crocodiles had developed in the valley. More often than not they fed off the fish or from the bodies of dead animals caught in the river's flow. After the times of flood, when the waters were murky and the fish dispersed, crocodiles took to the land at night and lay in ambush on game paths, waiting for puku or impala on their way to the river. The earth told the story of these hunts in the tracks left on the sand and in the great lunge marks and trails of blood where crocodiles dragged prey into the river.

Although crocodiles are shy by nature they could always be seen – from ancient giants to snappy youngsters – sunning themselves on the banks, their jaws held apart in a menacing grimace. Often when we walked along the river, beyond us there would be a sinister slithering noise across the sand at the water's edge, followed by the slightest of splashes.

Hippo also thrived in these waters, living harmoniously with one another when the river was full in the wet season, the bulls fighting to the death for territory as the waters receded. Little Boy and Little Girl had seen hippos at Londolozi, but never in such numbers. While terrified of the croc, the hippo fascinated them. Both of them lay under a bush watching from afar, frustrated that the size of these lumbering creatures prevented them from making closer investigation.

The bird life around the river was rich and varied. Flocks of stork soared down its length, following its winding course, their long spindly legs stretched as in a ballet behind them. On the flood plains, crowned cranes collected, their plaintive call like that of a crying child in the stillness of the early morning. A host of waders flitted and fished at the water's edge, pecking at the offerings the river brought them. Sandpiper stilts and plovers, with their especially adapted bills and feet, waited patiently for their catch or pursued it in hurried little runs across the shallows. Pelicans fished in flocks, filling their bright yellow pouches with their catch. Every now and then a solitary goliath heron, slate grey on its back with rich rufus underpants, flew downstream, the sound of its slow wing beats echoing down the valley. Egyptian geese squabbled over territory at the edges of the water and every now and then geometric formations of white-faced ducks or spur-winged geese filled the sky.

Flocks of red-billed queleas fascinated the cubs. Suddenly on the horizon, a column of smoke would appear as hosts of birds swarmed past, creating a great rushing noise, deafening in its volume. Then, abruptly, the flock moved off at a tangent, altering its tenor and rhythm as distinctly as a new movement in a symphony. Finding a richly seeded patch of grass, the flock would settle and a silence would hover for a few beats until the birds rose to the sky again. As one they were gone once more in a blast of sound. The energy of so many thousands of creatures moving over his head threw Little Boy into a spin. He launched himself at the flock as it settled or rose, not targeting any bird in particular. Little Girl in her prim way stuck to her classic stalk-and-pounce method. Neither had any success that we were aware of.

Our filming gear was always with us on our walks for documentation purposes, as it had been at Londolozi before the big work of the feature film. We filmed the cubs' antics opportunistically, each walk producing its own unexpected story or an aspect of the Luangwa Valley. The glare flashing off the stretches of sand flood plains in the valley made the light too harsh for filming for most of the day. At sunrise and sunset, when the light fell obliquely, a golden sheen drenched everything, enhancing it with a living glow. All life was surrounded by a halo of vibrating energy. Perhaps it was some mineral in the sands of the flood plains kicking back a reflection, or some trick of altitude or latitude. Each sunset and sunrise was an occasion, vast and biblical in its grandeur. The surreal effect of this light combined with our sense of isolation in the wilderness with two leopard cubs enhanced my feeling that we were in some lost Eden, in a dimensional warp, out of step with the linear progression of time.

One evening we gave Little Boy and Little Girl an impala carcass to eat. We were filming shots of them practising the stalk, the pounce and the killing bite to the neck. Little Boy lost interest and strolled off across the sandbank. Rays of the setting sun slanted across his body, highlighting the natural amber sheen of his coat. It gleamed with such intensity that he looked like a sculpture cast in bronze or fashioned from beaten enamel. He looked archetypal as he stood there in the afterglow of sunset, the subtle strength of his muscles understated in his easy stride, his shoulders thick and his neck arched with power. As I watched him, it was easy to understand how some cultures deified the leopard. Little Boy looked so otherworldly in that moment that I myself saw clearly the divine in him.

We continued writing up the daily events in the cubs' lives. From the very beginning, I had the team record their individual experiences with Little Boy and Little Girl and we would meet fortnightly to collate the data and discuss observations. This research included the documentation of physiological, behavioural and developmental detail, and then it went beyond this. What I was really after was the particularity of each relationship with Little Boy and Little Girl. Anything and everything the cubs shared with each one of us with our personal responses, feelings and interpretations was valid comment. As we all had a unique relationship with the cubs, we might harvest collectively the subtler messages and information coming from Little Boy and Little Girl.

While my observations specifically explored the more esoteric areas of communication and the nature of our relationship with the cubs, I was curious to find in the notes of others, among the narrative and developmental detail, the frequency of phrases such as 'It's like Little Girl reads your mind,' or 'Little Girl looks at you as if she understands your words.' Many other references pointed to their mind work and psychic agility.

Our work with the cubs was experiential. We were not attempting science in the mainstream sense, which holds that everything about ourselves and other animals, our mental and physical behaviour, can be explained reductively. Our experience with Mother Leopard, now our relationship with Little Boy and Little Girl, was more in character with what I understand is described in Japanese culture as 'kyokan'. Kyokan validates as science the process of learning and observation through a relationship of reciprocity formed with the subject of the study. This idea seemed to fit more comfortably with what we were doing. JV, who had learnt from Mother Leopard, close to her and yet still from the distance of a Landrover, could now extend the boundaries of his knowledge because of the proximity with which he lived with Little Boy and Little Girl. For him, it was an abiding passion to push forward the frontiers of this knowledge, to record it on film and share it with a wider audience.

For me, it was the psyche of cats that fascinated and drove me. In our relationship with Little Boy and Little Girl lay an opportunity to work towards kinship with leopards.

For the record we did keep factual data on the cubs, their weights and measurements and other developmental milestones. When they were tiny it was a very wriggly affair. We borrowed the infant scale from the clinic at Londolozi and lured the cubs onto the scales with bits of meat. As they grew, lying in the weighing dish or standing up and wobbling didn't give us accuracy. We weighed ourselves on a larger scale while holding the cubs and then subtracted our own weight from the total. This method also ran a short course before the cubs' writhing resistance. Flailing claws forced us to abandon it.

The tape measure for nose-to-tail was a game. After the destruction of many tape measures, we substituted string that either stretched or was bitten into pieces. That was another exercise we abandoned. This pretty much brought our weight and measurement records to a close and it was only when we sedated the cubs for relocation from Londolozi that we were able to get accurate measurements again.

At one year old, Little Boy weighed 35 kg; the average given an adult male leopard was anything between 31 kg and 65 kg, with top weights being recorded at 90 kg. Little Girl weighed in at 25 kg, the average given for females was between 17 kg and 58 kg. Nevertheless, it was interesting to compare the information we did collect along the way with that in the textbooks. It was information like this that confirmed how very different individual leopards are from one another, illustrating conclusively that it is leopards' skill at adaptability that has ensured their survival.

Our notes were littered with esoteric pieces of information. For example, when JV was roughing it up with Little Girl in the sand at Londolozi, she bit him in the excitement of the moment. It was a neat, precise bite and we were able to measure the wound on his foot, enabling us to say that at age 10 months, a young female leopard named Little Girl of Londolozi had a width of canines measuring four centimetres.

As we moved from the wet season of summer into the dry season of autumn and winter, we began to see thin plumes of poachers' fires snaking into the sky from remote parts of the Park. We would hear the echoes of rifle shot reverberating down the valley. After reporting the information on the radio to the game guards at park headquarters, an uncomfortable quiet would settle among us in camp, as even in a tenuous way, just by being human, we felt in part guilty.

The rationale of having the game guards Robert and Tennis stationed with us on T'Ingwe Island was for them to monitor our project. There was another reason for their presence, and that was to act as an outpost in the war against poaching. They utilised our presence as a deterrent and our radio to report sightings to the game scouts' base camp.

Prior to the sixties, the Luangwa Valley was renowned for its vast herds of elephant and populations of black rhino. Since then, it has been poached mercilessly. The elephant herds are decimated and black rhino all but extinct. It was a pathetic sight watching the elephants move down the valley in single family groups; a mother, maybe two, with one or two youngsters in tow, rather than in robust herds – the way elephants choose to live. It was as if the understanding had spread among their species that their whereabouts were less easily detected if they went about their daily lives quietly and in small numbers. I felt shame in the presence of these refugee family groups.

The seasons in the Luangwa Valley rolled by even more quickly than further south at Londolozi. From one day to the next it seemed, the leaves of the mopani trees yellowed and fell and the levels of the Luangwa River dropped daily before our eyes.

The main body of the river shrank back to the permanent watercourse, which cut its path between the south bank of T'Ingwe Island and the GMA. To the north, the side that faced the National Park, the water became knee-deep in parts with thin ribbons of deeper water winding through the sandbank. In time, game would migrate across the stretch between the island and the mainland. Both banks were now richly fringed with new grass.

Little Boy showed the gallantry of a sub-adult male leopard, with his preference for the route to the north. Herds of zebra, puku and impala moved to and from the island with the seasonal ebb and flow. The cubs instinctively picked up the clues to this natural migration. Little Girl was still wary of any large body of water, including the paddling pools to the west. This was Little Boy's soccer, water polo and cooling-off terrain. She held back slightly on the walks to the north, where the waters were still treacherous. Both cubs showed a sensitivity to the dangers of crocodile, perhaps recalling the Big Crocodile Battle at Londolozi during filming. They showed due respect for the watery habitat of the Luangwa Valley.

In this northern area, Little Boy made his first formal Zambian hunt. A small genet was sniffing around in the grass as we walked by early one morning. Little Boy's response was so quick that he had the genet by the back of the neck before even he realised what had happened. A genet is a feisty little creature and when it struggled, hissing and spitting viciously, he dropped it and it made its getaway into the tangle of undergrowth. Little Boy was after it like a flash, leaping around animatedly as he did when after something in the long grass that he couldn't properly see, to pinpoint it by its movement. Perhaps he hoped he might land on it from above. Little Girl joined in the chase, but the genet was long gone. Spurred on by his near success, Little Boy returned to the spot, believing he had found fertile hunting grounds.

He was right, for soon enough small herds of puku moved across to T'Ingwe Island. The males are fiercely territorial, not an uncommon trait in antelope, but what is peculiar to the puku is the style of its defence. Challenged or scared off from where he is holding court, waiting for the females of the herd to pass through his home range, a male puku will run from danger, circle the area in a fairly tight loop and take up his position in exactly the same place as he was before. Over and over again the cubs played a game of chase that never ended.

Puku are found predominantly in Zambia, with small populations in Botswana and Zimbabwe. They have a natural affinity for water and often head for the shallows when pursued by predators. They attempt to escape using the spray thrown up by their hooves as a screen along with a repertoire of other escape manoeuvres such as flailing hooves, twisting, swerving and feinting. Their delicacy and grace belies their speed and agility. While we were all keen to see the cubs start hunting antelope, we were anxious about Little Boy's overestimation of his abilities. He might overreach himself and tangle with the lethal horns of the puku.

That morning, Little Girl wandered off from camp independently. Of late she enjoyed being on her own in the trees, harmonising her energy with that flowing around her. There were times when the image of her brother suddenly came into her mind and she felt an urgency to be with him. This impulse that distracted her from all else happened that morning as she lay in the branches of the kigelia tree. Carefully she scanned the middle distance, then climbed down the trunk and headed off to the north where she had seen her brother heading. From some distance she heard the high-pitched whistle of a puku. Increasing her pace, she followed the cry to its source.

She came onto the edge of the clearing and saw her brother gathering himself to stalk a young puku. Instinctively, she dropped to the ground, froze and watched. She saw what Little Boy hadn't seen. The mother puku was moving in from his blind side to defend her offspring. Before Little Girl could move, there was a sickening thud. Abandoning her customary caution she ran forward. Her heart hoped that Little Boy had brought down the fawn before the puku mother had reached him. But no, through the dust that rose she could see her brother's body flung through the air. In the confusion of alarm calls and panic, the remaining puku scattered and circled. But there was no sign of her brother, only an ominous silence.

She found Little Boy lying tangled in a bush, blood flowing from the corner of his mouth, his eyes closed. She knew directly that he wasn't asleep because of the silence of his thoughts. She ran over to him and licked his face and when he didn't respond, she paced up and down. Little Boy was gone and she was alone. She swallowed rapidly once or twice and then a mournful cry came surging up from the depths of her being.

As if in response, a slight rustle came from the bush where Little Boy lay. He sat up, blinked, shook his head and stared at his sister vacantly. In her shocked state, she wasn't sure if it was relief that swelled in her or anger. She sat discreetly, with her back stiff, her mouth pursed, pushing her whiskers forward. She deliberately looked the other way and ignored him.

Little Boy, Master of the Universe, thought it had been the perfect hunt. He'd been lying under the cover of a cluster of ebony saplings, watching the puku feed on the grass shoots fringing the sandbank. To his great delight, a young puku separated itself from its mother. The planets themselves had lined up in a favourable aspect. What Little Boy didn't know was that the moon was in Aries, that aspect of great delusion which made him feel invincible and walk with that extra bounce. The young puku – as if under his hypnotic spell – headed straight towards him. Down he sank, low to the ground in a crouch. Little Boy's thigh muscles twitched with eagerness. How admiring his sister would have been of his preparation.

Slowly, the young puku moved closer and closer. Little Boy landed perfectly on the fawn. He grappled into position on its back to wrestle his prey to the ground. Down it went. Just as he felt his canines breaking the surface of the puku's skin at the throat, something hit him like a rock and spun him bodily into the air. The last image in Little Boy's mind before darkness closed in was the horns of the mother puku.

As he opened his eyes, Little Boy found himself lying in an undignified heap in a bush, covered in bits of dry leaves and thorn. The salty taste of blood in his mouth, a ringing noise in his ears and his vision unfocused. He blinked then shook his head vigorously, trying to settle the movement of everything swaying about him. Not far off, the puku began to feed once more, lifting their heads periodically to stare at him. He looked cautiously around him and there, some yards off, he saw his sister sitting primly, her back stiffened, looking the other way.

I celebrated a birthday on T'Ingwe Island. The guests at my party included Little Boy and Little Girl. That day we followed the usual ritual of adventuring – exploring the sandbanks where the cubs investigated the news of the day written in the sand, the grasses and the shrubs. As sunset reddened the sky we drank a toast in authentic glass tumblers. I took in the vastness of Luangwa Valley and was overcome by the privilege of commemorating my birthday in one of Nature's last refuges in the company of our leopard friends. Such an exquisite and fleeting moment seems unreal in remembering it.

Gulam Patel from Tundwe Lodge made the journey to T'Ingwe Island to spend the evening with us. He brought a box of fresh produce from Lusaka that elevated him to the status of a saint, as we'd been eating from tins.

The magic of my birthday grew as the sky darkened and the heavens came alive, lit by infinite stars – my celestial birthday candles. I could feel the rough sand from the beach on my bare feet. In the distance, hippo grunted in the river and the whistles of the plovers travelled on the currents of the night air. The campfire crackled softly, its flame drawing all of us into its depths. The conversation was gentle and profound. The stuff that comes of freedom, fire, friends and being close to nature. JV strummed on his guitar and before long he and Gulam were singing Jim Reeves love songs. In the night sky the two dogs, Canis Major and Minor, faithfully followed at the heels of Orion. The light of the flames flickering across our faces reminded me of our first campfire with the cubs a year before, when we began this journey with them. Another dimension had opened up as I recalled with joy the experiences and insights we had shared with these wild creatures, soon to move out of our lives.

# CHAPTER SEVEN

# *Hambani kahle, zingwe ezincane*

*Go well, little leopards*

We knew that Little Boy and Little Girl would leave us. When their leaving did come, it was too soon. It caught us off balance, as we'd been lulled into the daily rhythm of life on T'Ingwe Island.

There were signs – a restlessness, a rebuttal where once there might have been a welcoming greeting. With it was a silent plea not to insist on things being the way they had been. Little Boy, ever congenial, was polite and accommodating when we persisted in looking for an affectionate rub or a game of stalk-and-pounce. In Little Girl's eyes there was a cast of pain. Some deeper knowledge was causing conflict within her. It was as if she knew what had to be, but in her dilemma didn't want to aggrieve us.

The day began like almost any other. It was April and even as the sun edged its way into the sky, the heat and humidity descended like a blanket. The cubs were lethargic and kept close to camp. As the afternoon cooled off, their energies rose.

Little Boy led the walk. He was deliberate in the direction he chose and headed directly towards the river, with Little Girl following close behind. Together, Little Boy and Little Girl lay on the sandbank, Little Boy looking intently at the water. Quite suddenly, he got up and went to the water's edge. He stepped in and waded a bit, stopped, turned around and looked back. Then, with resolve, he continued into the water and kept on walking.

He went slowly and purposefully, and reaching a deeper channel, swam, turning constantly to look back towards camp, taking a full 15 or 20 minutes to cross the stretch of water that lay between T'Ingwe Island and the far bank. Little Girl didn't take her eyes off him for a second. She sat alert at the edge of the water, her back stiff. When her brother reached the far side of the river, he emerged from the water, shook himself vigorously, groomed briefly and then disappeared behind the sandbank.

The moment he was out of sight, Little Girl rose and moved closer to the water's edge. Her nervousness of a large stretch of water was evident in her pacing at the edge. She realised she had to swim across channels of deep water to reach Little Boy and in her dilemma, hesitated. Then, reluctantly, she stepped in. She scanned the water for crocodiles and then looked imploringly back towards Karin, who was with the cubs at the time. She kept looking back as she went further and further into the water. After a short while, Little Boy reappeared, calling to his sister in a strangely high-pitched tone. He came to the far edge of the water and called again, more agitated this time, then disappeared behind the sandbank.

Taking even longer than Little Boy, Little Girl crossed the river, heading for where she had seen her brother, her anxiety expressed in the sharp angularity of her movements. Emerging on the other side, she shook herself as much to get rid of the water as to shake off the horror of crossing the stream. Then, she too disappeared behind the same sandbank.

There was a brief moment of silence as Karin sat uncomprehending on our side of the river. The cubs had never done this before. At first she was frightened that she might lose them if she didn't follow them, but she was alone and crocodiles were everywhere. Then, slowly, understanding filtered through her bewilderment. Just then, Little Boy and Little Girl re-emerged on the far side, walked briefly side-by-side along the riverbank and then vanished into the bush. Karin called and called but there was no response. The cubs had made their first attempt at independence.

It was to be their first night out alone.

JV, Elmon and I were downstream at camp at the time and hurried to T'Ingwe Island when we received the news. Some hours had passed, with no sign of Little Boy and Little Girl. Had they lost their nerve when faced with re-crossing the river? Had they lost their way? We took meat across to the other side of the river and walked up and down, calling.

There were moments when I felt a distinct presence. Perhaps the cubs were watching us, practising the art of concealment. They would let us bumble around blindly and suddenly reveal themselves with studied nonchalance. That was it. That was what was going on. We would find them soon. But this time there was nothing. As evening fell, we withdrew to our camp. That night, despite the grand orchestra of the African night, a silence fell, as solemn as a requiem, as we lay unsleeping in our tents.

For days there was no trace of Little Boy or Little Girl, no tracks in the sand to tell of their intentions. The bush rang with possibilities – francolins alarming, vervets calling and the chirruping of the sun squirrels indicating the presence of a predator – but we found nothing. We followed up on all the clues sent to us on the bush network – rustling sounds in the tree tops, light crackling of a tread on dry grass, twigs snapping in the undergrowth. But no cubs.

I found myself floundering, one moment feeling a surge of pride at the two young creatures stepping forward on their own, then fearful at having to stand by as they followed their destiny. In our limited way, we had tried to convey to Little Boy and Little Girl that this moment would come. But could they truly have understood what independence meant, until the hormonal changes took place within their bodies and the urge for freedom took their spirits? Even though we humans could imagine the future, we weren't really prepared for this parting. The sense of mystery and wonder at what we had shared became heightened. The privilege of living in companionship with two leopard cubs had been awesome, and we didn't want it to end.

Some days later, as if from nowhere, Little Boy's tracks appeared on the bank of a small peninsula between T'Ingwe Island and the mainland, leading into the water where the cubs had crossed. But no tracks emerged on the other side. It was a grim discovery. Had he tried to return to the island and been taken by crocodiles? Graham was convinced he had. JV and Elmon were non-committal until they found more evidence. Karin and I held onto hope, as women always do. Privately I wept, frustrated that we had been unable to help them in this critical rite of passage. I was unable to accept that this was a process they had to face alone.

But the crocodiles loomed larger and more sinister than ever, and as they lay on the riverbank in the sun with their mouths ajar, I imagined some secret passing silently between them. In the slow, waking hours of the night, the hyenas' maniacal giggles sounded eerie and derisive. Even the familiar grunting of the hippos seemed to ridicule my wish for Little Boy and Little Girl to return. It seemed that danger lay in every shadow and behind every tree.

Our team was in disarray; our hopes of locating the cubs or knowing what happened were pinned on the language of the sand. Elmon and JV scoured the area, looking for signs relayed by the earth. After some searching, they found tracks that swung sideways from the water near the point of entry. Had Little Boy changed his course? Hope surged.

The talk among us was exhilarated. After all, the independence of Little Boy and Little Girl was the moment we had been working towards. 'They've done it!' said JV, grinning. 'They've gone and done it!'

But a note of bravado tinged his excitement, and the way his eyes searched the horizon suggested an inner uncertainty.

It was a time for faith in Nature. The human need to know was difficult for us to deal with. To love them but to remain detached – this was the great lesson that the cubs had taught us during our time together. It was being tested.

And then one night, without warning, Little Boy reappeared in the camp. We were overjoyed to see him and fussed over him excessively, but Little Boy was changed. He was restless and cried repeatedly in a distressing, high-pitched way. Nothing could soothe him, not even the offer of a good meal. We strung up meat in a tree where he could eat in privacy and safety, and we let him know we were available for companionship or protection. All night long, the roar of lions proclaiming territory echoed up and down the valley.

The next morning we were out of camp before sunrise. Little Boy was keeping his distance, lying up in the thicket on the far side of the island. We struggled to contain the urge to be close, busying ourselves around the camp. Every so often, one of us made a furtive visit to the thicket to see if he was still there. We moved about cautiously, not wanting to send him off again. It was difficult to behave in any ordinary way.

And then the following day a joyful sight met us. Little Girl was back. She had joined Little Boy during the night. As if to tell of her newfound independence, she had hunted a genet. Its half-eaten carcass lay close to the thicket where we found them.

The cubs made the thicket their base. They would not come back into the camp or into their boma at night. Respectfully, we stayed in our camp and the cubs kept to their side of the island. A tacit understanding. These were the days of transition in the dispersal process. Accepting this focused us on the magical moments of this period of grace.

Little Boy was overly playful in these days, his behavior regressing to his carefree cubhood days. Fluctuating between dependence and independence, he was throwing off the mantle of his newfound adulthood and composure. He leapt around in the branches of the trees, more the clown than ever, tumbling comically to the ground as the slender branches gave way. He played the somersault game, the slender branch game, and the ambush game. A note of nostalgia echoed softly between us, a silent collusion.

There were days when we didn't see the cubs at all, no matter how long and hard we searched. Then the chill would grip at the heart again. Was this the final moment? There were times too when there was a strong sense of their presence, but we wouldn't see them.

Little Girl, surprisingly, joined in the fun, abandoning herself to silliness. But so deep and abiding was her respect for proper leopard behaviour that before long she reined herself in, sitting with her back held primly, her mood slightly aloof. She spent long hours up a kigelia tree, sleeping or in meditative mien. Fondly, we imagined that her expedition into independence had exhausted her, confirming our hopes that it wasn't time yet for the final parting. When she did come to us, she was more affectionate than ever, delicately tapping with her paw on our arms or thigh to let us know she was there. These were precious, encapsulated days, made surreal with the intensity of our knowing.

About a month after Little Boy first crossed the river, we were gathered on the beach. The atmosphere glowed with that otherworldly luminosity of the late afternoon sun. We'd walked to Little Boy's favorite splash pools and paused to watch the sun set behind the Ndchene Hills. As the sun sank below the horizon, the doon palms on the opposite bank fell into an exotic skyline silhouette. I watched Little Boy as he moved across the sand in front of me, flicking his sturdy paws loosely at the wrist. He was still as plump as a butterball, but underneath his neck and shoulders were broad and powerful. There was a new pride in his bearing. The setting sun shone on his face. There had always been amiability in his expression, but for the first time, I detected something new there which flickered and then passed. It seemed to me a hardening in his look, the cool detachment of an adult leopard. Little Boy was no longer a cub. The moment held itself briefly, then lapsed as he fell to playing ambush. It was his time-honoured cue for the fun to begin.

That evening was to be the last time we ever saw Little Boy.

For the next few days, Little Girl remained on the island alone, her mood tense and distracted. She was stressed and called in a whining tone, occasionally making low grunting noises. She looked repeatedly at the river with haunted eyes. What was the message in her searching and her agitated movements to and from the river's edge? We were unable to soothe her pining.

Once again we were sensitive to every alarm call in the bush, raising hopes of Little Boy's return. Little Girl continued to stay out at night. She was slight in build and appeared so vulnerable without the presence of her brother. Would her attachment to Little Boy be a drawback to her own quest for freedom?

One night we heard lions calling from close by, and went the following morning to the thicket to reassure her. The scuffmarks indicated the lions had chased Little Girl. She was safe in the kigelia tree but was frightened and on edge. She kept her distance from us as the days passed. Across the space between us, our hearts ached as we watched her spirits sinking lower and lower.

A week after Little Boy left, Little Girl made an attempt to cross the river on her own. A troop of baboons shrieking from the trees on the far bank scared her and she retreated to the island. The impala carcass we hung in the kigelia tree she chose for her safety, remained untouched. She looked thinner and weaker each time we saw her, her eyes hollow and strained.

And then, she too left us.

The only messages after that were tracks in the sand. We found them everywhere and caught glimpses of leopards at every turn, unsure of what was real and what was imagined. We heard wild leopards calling with their strange rasping cough in the early hours of half-light and found clear tracks of a large male we thought might be the territorial male. At the rate Little Boy and Little Girl were growing, we were afraid we would soon be unable to tell theirs apart. Elmon and JV's tracking skills remained a tenuous link with the new life that Little Boy and Little Girl had embarked on.

We kept the camp running on T'Ingwe Island in case Little Boy or Little Girl returned or gave us some indication that they needed us. We wandered around listlessly without any focus, finally packing up. Our community, once vibrant and purposeful, had lost its heartbeat. The unmet expectation of an ambush from behind a tent flap or the tufts of grass behind the showers was a sad reminder of what once had been.

My human way of loving was getting in the way of closure. The longing I felt haunted me deep inside, where nothing could reach it. I felt an anger at this way of parting, which I accepted in theory, but found so difficult. I begged the Universe for some sign, some way of knowing, but was met by the empty silence that hung over the camp like a pall. Uncomfortable, this joy and this sadness. In the wild, a leopard mother seeks her newly independent cubs out intermittently, but we could not do that. If only they would return one more time. I bargained with the Universe. I was like a child who avoids walking on the cracks of a pavement in the superstitious hope that some wish would come true.

We withdrew from T'Ingwe Island. Karin and Graham returned to South Africa, where both were hospitalised with severe malaria to add to the misery of their loss. JV, Elmon and I stayed on in the Luangwa Valley and, some six weeks later, returned to T'Ingwe Island. We had no particular purpose in mind, a need for closure perhaps, simply to revisit the place that held so much meaning; some hope that the earth would bear a message. We walked up through the park and crossed to the north bank of the island. An eerie stillness lay over what had formerly been the campsite.

The expectation of ambush had not left me. It was palpable in its absence. I kept glancing over my shoulder. Would Little Boy hurl himself at my ankles, leaping from behind a bush, or would I glimpse his bottom wriggling in the air from behind a solitary clump of grass? For a long moment, I distinctly felt Little Girl's presence as we searched the bare and silent patches of sand. If I searched long and hard enough in her old hiding places, would I find some news of her? In that limbo between loss and acceptance, it was still too soon to gain comfort from memories. We could only hold faith that Nature would be benevolent to these courageous creatures.

There were so many questions that remained unanswered. That was the way it was with leopards, so many hints and guesses. Hadn't Mother Leopard taught us that? Little Boy and Little Girl's story confirmed the lesson. Mother Leopard had set up a wave, which caught us all in its momentum and was continued in Little Boy and Little Girl's crossing into the twilight zone of interaction between human and wild animal.

We had learnt so much of what it was to be human and what it was to be leopard. In this distinction, the perennial wisdom that we were all part of a greater scheme. A delicate yet powerful moment.

I sat under Little Girl's favourite kigelia tree, lost in a sense of wonder at the lives of these two leopards I had come to think of as my little brother and sister. I retraced their lives up to their final metamorphosis as wild leopards.

What if I were to predict the cubs' trajectory after leaving us, drawing on our experience of leopards? Or, in the tradition of the Shamans, I were to journey in a parallel reality and see Little Boy and Little Girl's lives from there? How would it be?

JV and Elmon walked around, half-heartedly looking for tracks on the ground. They felt the finality as keenly as I did. There had been a transformation in all of us, a great internal shift beyond our previous experience of relationships and of love.

Then I heard Elmon call. The triumphant tone had me on my feet in seconds and I raced across to him. There, in a patch of sand where our tents had been, were two sets of tracks, barely visible. He was convinced that they belonged to Little Boy and Little Girl, walking side by side. Had the cubs made the concession to our human fragility? I fell to my knees in the sand with gratitude. Little Boy and Little Girl had made it across the divide. My vision of their tracks in the sand blurred. I cried for the joy, the loss and for that mystical world we shared.

\* \* \*

Little Boy was running scared. His chest heaved with exertion and the pounding of his heart thudded inside his head. His nostrils flared and burned and a searing pain shot through his lungs. He stumbled momentarily. Then he regained his stride and limped on. He moved through the thick bush with short, deliberate strides and where the undergrowth thinned, he broke into short bursts of speed. Even though his shoulders ached with exhaustion, he dared not stop moving. Little Boy knew he was compromising the silence. Even the undergrowth conspired against him as the pods of the river bean bush cracked explosively when he trod on them.

A patch of mopani forest lay ahead, its slim trees now bare. The fallen leaves carpeted the forest floor with a tapestry of golden-ochre and russet. Little Boy picked his way through the slender trunks of the young trees, wincing at the sharp crackle of the dry leaves and snapping twigs. For a moment, he regretted his choice of direction. He had chosen the forest, hoping that its dappled light would conceal him as it flickered over his form, breaking up the outline of his body, the colour of his coat merging with that of the leaves as he escaped from the terror of that morning.

Uncertain of his way, Little Boy thought of jumping up a tree to get a wider view, but his recent misadventure with tree reconnaissance put him off. He was not comfortable with breaking whatever cover he had at his disposal. However, the urge to see how the land lay was stronger, so he sloped cautiously up a termite mound and scanned the area. To the west lay a wide band of tangled shrub and long grass. His preference was to stick to the cover, but inner guidance directed him southwards.

Little Boy was in survival mode. Responses to the myriad choices he had faced since the terror had flown unbidden to his mind. Little Boy was experiencing a surge of flight adrenalin.

He'd been moseying around the edges of the riverine thicket, not far from where he had left Little Girl a few moon cycles before. He was looking for something on which to redeploy his energies after the lizard had escaped into the cleft of a young ebony tree. The hunt had been going well, when it had been cut short by the disappearance of his prey. Then a scraping sound alerted him to the presence of something moving through the bush. He sprang lightly up the ebony. Time stopped. Not ten paces off was a leopard the size of a lion. The territorial male whose presence Little Boy had scented during the last few weeks.

The leopard was dragging the carcass of a puku and the weight of the prey was absorbing his energy and attention. The leopard shifted the carcass, massive paws pushing at the earth, his forelegs stiff, straddling the dead weight, shoulder muscles bunching as he arched his neck to clear the carcass from the ground.

In one cold moment, Little Boy realised he was up the tree into which the territorial male was about to hoist his kill. Unable to move, he stared as the leopard shifted closer and closer to the tree. His domed head and shoulders loomed larger and larger until they filled Little Boy's vision. Then came the dreadful moment. The territorial male looked up into the tree to steady himself and his gaze locked with the terrified eyes of Little Boy. He drew his lips back in a snarl and his growl reverberated in his throat, impacting on Little Boy like a physical blow. The eyes were yellow and had a malevolent glint to them. There was murderous intent written there.

Initially, it was the sheer size and bristling power that shocked Little Boy. Then he saw the scars across the head that told of success in many a violent encounter. In the same second that fear paralysed his mind, the rush of adrenalin surged through his body. Instinct saved him. Little Boy's timing could not have been more perfect. In the nanosecond that it took for the territorial male to react, Little Boy flung himself headlong from the tree and bolted, the element of surprise giving him some advantage.

Little Boy hit the ground hard, the impact knocking the air from his lungs. The territorial male's vacillation over whether to leave his hard-won puku kill unguarded, gave Little Boy another few metres. Then the leopard launched himself. Little Boy could hear the panting of hot breath and could almost feel the bite to the back of his neck. The earth shook as the adult leopard thundered after him, the tip of the fur at the back of his body alive to the closeness. Little Boy had agility and suppleness, the natural result of a cubhood enhanced by fighting games with his sister. This lightness gave Little Boy the edge in the chase through the undergrowth. It seemed as though he were flying, his feet barely touching the ground. For what seemed eternity, Little Boy felt the territorial male close at his heels. He twisted and turned, using every manoeuvre he knew, and just when he thought he was gaining ground, he slipped in a turn.

Little Boy felt the smack on his right flank and the razor-like talons ripping through his flesh, the dewclaw hooking under his paw and, like a grappling iron, throwing him off his feet. The impact of the blow flung Little Boy upwards and into the air. The earth became the sky and the sky the earth as he spun and then hit the ground with a dull thud, rolling onto his back with the territorial male on top of him. Another powerful blow to the side of his head and Little Boy knew he was staring death in the face. Above him loomed the scarred head, ears pulled flat as his head snaked from side to side, his lips drawn back, exposing yellowing canines stained at the gums by the blood of the prey. There was aggression in his eyes as they narrowed to slits, the skin of his face folding into a snarl.

As Little Boy raised his paws pathetically to protect his throat, a look of hesitation flickered in the other leopard's eyes. Something passed between them which Little Boy would only come to understand later – the universal principle that to yield is to prevail. In his submission, Little Boy's life was saved. In the eloquent body-talk of leopards, lying on his back, his underbelly and throat exposed, was Little Boy's final gesture of appeasement. The territorial male would hurt, but could not kill this youngster, who had not challenged his tenure and whose every indication was that he wanted to get out of his way. He stood up, raised his head with the elegance of unspoken victory and gazed with indifference into the middle distance. He wanted to hoist his puku kill into the ebony before the hyenas shuffling around the edge of the woodland were alert to the carcass.

Little Boy ran. It was as if he were free of any physical exertion as his body responded in flight, in a state of grace where time was meaningless.

Hours later, Little Boy plodded heavily, a desperate animal, his head hung low and swinging awkwardly from side to side. His tail dragged, he was barely able to raise the tip. The usual supple roll of his shoulders was spasmodic and jerked with tension and the ache of exhaustion. He longed for a shady bush where he could lie up and recompose himself. He'd been running for the past few hours. A leopard is not a creature designed for long-distance running. With short, powerful limbs and a low centre of gravity, its physique has been honed for short bursts of speed, for powerful leaps and agility in trees. Even its paws, well equipped with retractable claws, are committed to killing, not to running. Little Boy had depleted all his reserves.

The heat of the day slowed him. He longed for the cool evening air. Little Boy needed to see the stars in the sky, to find the messages of light so he could get his bearings. Their familiarity in the sky each night was reassuring. He would lie gazing at them, fascinated by their vibration.

When Little Boy emerged from the mopani forest, he slowed his pace. He brushed up against a grewia bush and his heart lurched – the unmistakable scent of the territorial male leopard. It all came together now. It was the scent he had picked up when he and Little Girl had first crossed the river from T'Ingwe Island. It lingered around the riverine bushes in an ill-defined way. Little Boy at 12 months had dismissed the scent, even though his instinct had made him recoil when he first smelled it. This casualness with the law exasperated Little Girl so that her whiskers would pull right forward; such was the tension around her mouth. Little Boy thought of her fondly now, desperately. In the last few hours, something of what she had tried to impress on him, of caution and analysis, was beginning to have meaning. He should have known better. Just before he had leapt into that ebony tree, he'd picked up the scent again. More pungent.

Scuff marks around on the ground help to spread scent and confirm it, as do the scratchings in trees. The second time Little Boy smelled the scent he had wanted to move away, to withdraw, but he had gone after the lizard instead. Failure to comply with the law of leopards had nearly caused Little Boy's death. It would be his last cubhood indulgence.

He stood alongside the grewia bush, the scent of the territorial male in his nostrils. Before bolting, he sniffed at the bush again. The scent was faint. He was probably at the edges of the territorial male's area. He wasn't safe yet. But neither was he in any immediate danger.

Little Boy moved on, more sensitive to the scent of the undergrowth. An angle of sunlight slanting through the trees brought a jumble of thoughts and images. He remembered his first encounter with a wild leopard during his cubhood at Londolozi. A female leopard had conveyed a message to him that he was unable to fathom. She circled him and lay down before him repeatedly, a kind of rumbling in her throat, halfway between a purr and a chirp. There was a clear invitation there, but for what? And that taunting arrogance in her demeanour, haughty, challenging. There'd been no mystery about the look in the territorial male's eye. The sunlight fell on other incidents. The Leguvaan Kill, The Great Crocodile Battle. The Puku Mishap – how he'd misread that situation.

Then he thought about the day he'd crossed the river and left the people.

As he swam, he felt the energy patterns of some living thing in the water. Crocodiles? He swam as fast as he could. He had expected Little Girl to be right behind him, as she usually was. Had she not grasped the significance of this day? He went back some way and called repeatedly for her with urgency from the other side. And then finally she had come across, strung out and reproachful.

His sister soon entered into the spirit of the adventure as they began exploring. Firstly, they needed to attend to reconnaissance. For Little Girl, it was the most necessary of leopard behaviours.

At first the cubs tumbled around as they had always done, but soon that strange and new urge to move dominated. Little Girl had been more reluctant than before to follow him. So they had stayed in the area for some days, adventuring together sometimes and sometimes alone, linking up, moving towards and away from each other. The invisible cord between them stretched but still held them together. It would always be that way.

Little Boy's mind returned to the present. His ears were flattened and still swivelled rapidly to catch any sounds of pursuit. He longed to lie up, to regain his equilibrium, to groom himself, to regain his composure. His coat was bedraggled and shot through with burrs and bits of leaves. Broken thorns stabbed the pads of his feet and his back leg ached where claws had slashed through his flesh. Blood matted his coat. Little Boy was usually a well-groomed leopard, not fastidious like Little Girl, but careful in a casual kind of way.

Something powerful had happened outside of linear time. His encounter had compressed a vastness into an instant. In that nuclear moment, Little Boy had passed from one state of being to another. He had been pushed to the limits and at this extreme, the will to survive – that which makes a creature truly wild – was born.

Little Boy came across a pool of water. The temptation to rush headlong into the coolness of its embrace was overwhelming. First, he waited in the cover while he listened and watched. Then he moved forward, drank deeply and sank bodily into the water. It washed over his body, easing the pain in his limbs, the pressure on the pads of his feet and the ache in his shoulders. He loved the magical way water seeped through his fur. The water cooled him as the moonlight did.

For a brief, good-humoured moment brought on by the relief of the water, did Little Boy think to himself that he had displayed good timing in response to the attack? Or did he understand that he had been truly chastened?

A quarter moon rising in the sky would be to Little Boy's advantage, a low light in which to make good of the long journey. The stars began to shine: Orion on the western horizon, its super giant Betelgeuse glowing red; Scorpius rising in the east; ahead, prominent in the Milky Way, Centaurus.

Little Boy emerged from the water with grace and walked to a vantage point on the river bank, exposing himself for a brief moment. He took in the scene, the picture of a young male leopard poised on the brink of adult life. His coat gleamed lustrous in the pale light of the moon. Silently, he slipped down the far side of the sandbank, merging with the shadows, and headed south. In front of him, was the South Luangwa National Park, a mosaic of vegetation stained inky blue and dark green in the afterglow. In the distance lay the Muchinga Hills, purple and rimmed by the rising moonlight. The low persistent hoot of a Skops owl echoed down the valley, answered by the grunts of a hippo from a pool in the river. Little Boy raised his head in silent acknowledgment to the emerging stars, and then moved on. Yes, thought Little Boy, this way ...

\* \* \*

High up in the leafy recesses of a mahogany tree on the north bank of the Luangwa River, Little Girl arched and let the stretch run sensuously through the muscles along her neck and spine. Then lightly and with perfect balance she dropped and lay in perfect repose, her body moulding to the sturdy bough and dangling loosely. Her eyes scanned the middle distance and, registering nothing of any immediate consequence, began to glaze over. The white tip of her tail twitched once or twice and then, resting her cheek lightly on her forearm, Little Girl closed her eyes.

That morning she had flushed a yellow-footed bush squirrel in the nearby thicket. She had gripped it by the throat, her canines sunk well into its spine, severing the chord and preventing the hapless creature from uttering the slightest cry to betray her success to the hyenas and jackals. Despite the pangs of hunger that had clawed at her stomach for the past day or two, she ate with her customary delicacy, first plucking clean the fur and meticulously opening the kill at its soft underbelly and working her way up the carcass with neatness and precision. A small meal with nothing to store for later. She scratched dirt over the remains of the fur and entrails and leapt lightly into the mahogany tree, where she groomed herself.

She had chosen well. During the cycle since the last full moon, the mahogany tree had become a friend. There was a comfortable sense of communion between them, a mutual recognition of some past-life elemental experience. The imposing 200-year-old tree had offered sanctuary to many leopards, but in Little Girl it recognised a truly arboreal spirit, one which drew power and balance from its sturdy rootedness deep into the earth, lightness and energy from the exalted reach of its branches into the sky. Although lions could manage the lower levels, the tree offered Little Girl defence if she retreated higher to the slender branches above. This tree was her safe haven. It would become her larder as she became a skilled hunter.

The tree was also her vantage point. Little Girl could see into the thicket beneath which edged onto a clearing. She would hunt the impala, puku and warthog that sought shade there. Far across the sandbanks, she could see in advance any danger that lay at the edge of the water. If she cast her gaze to the distance, she could see T'Ingwe Island. Never had she been so happy to find so accommodating a tree.

It was from this tree that she had seen the people cross the river and walk along the sandbank next to the water. They talked excitedly and pointed to the ground at the tracks around her usual drinking place. She heard them calling her name; soft faraway sounds that came to her on the wind, from another time and place. Once, they walked directly beneath her tree.

Even JV didn't see her, although he had an uncanny way of thinking along with her. Neither did Elmon, who always found the paths she walked without so much as putting his nose to the ground to scent the track. Gillian walked slowly behind them. Little Girl felt her longing and it confused her momentarily. She saw that Karin was distressed too. She was carrying food with her, but Little Girl wasn't hungry. She didn't feel at all well and stayed motionless on the bough that held her as she watched the people pass by, completely detached. It had been a moon cycle she never wanted to experience again.

What Little Boy had done had not come as a surprise to her. The upheaval in their lives when they first came to T'Ingwe Island sparked an uneasiness in both of them. Something had begun edging into her mind then, an unformed feeling of restlessness. Then one day, bold as ever, that brother of hers simply struck off without any forewarning.

She watched him plunge into the water, where he knew those glinty-eyed crocodiles lay in wait for the thirsty and the reckless. Then he swam without hesitation for the far bank where they had never been before. She fretted at the water's edge, imploring him to come back, but she recognised his frame of mind. She would have to react quickly or else be left behind. She hated and feared the murky depths and the unseen dangers lurking there. Momentarily she lost sight of Little Boy, and as panic threatened to overwhelm her, he reappeared from behind a sandbank and called her impatiently, ignoring her distress. She had no choice.

She crossed the river, senses jangling with fear, the danger of the water behind her and the unknown looming before her. Her mind shifted into an altered reality, her focus on the detail around her slipping in and out. Little Girl's memory of this time was vague and ill-defined, so stifled was it by anxiety; confused images of splashing water crocodiles slipping into the river from the sandbanks, Little Boy urging her on; the sound of the people calling her back.

For the next few cycles of the moon, she and Little Boy stayed close together, more bonded than ever. Together, they faced the challenges of this new place, Little Boy's certainty giving her the support she needed, a confidence that made her more expansive than her usual cautionary self. They explored the woodland around the edge of the river and even when they hunted lizards and frogs, he did not growl at her as he had always done when food was available.

Her brother still didn't show the dedication she felt he ought to in piecing together the information of the area. Though he was his usual good-natured self, occasionally she would see him sitting staring into the far distance at nothing in particular, lost in thoughts she didn't under-stand. Or he would pace up and down restlessly, yowling in a way that spoke of turmoil inside him.

In their wanderings and discoveries, they came across the scent at the base of the bush that edged onto the mopani forest. Other leopards. Little Boy recoiled at the scent, but was soon distracted and went off hunting. She lingered around the spot, searching her mind for meaning. In places the scent was more pungent than in others. Over the days she began to discern a pattern. Something drew her to it. She was intrigued by it but its true message would only come to her later with sexual maturity.

One day, without explanation and as suddenly as before, Little Boy struck off again from the new place on the mainland and headed straight back for T'Ingwe camp across the river. At first, Little Girl was tempted to follow, but felt disinclined to leave the new area where she felt a grow-ing sense of belonging. She returned to the mahogany tree, where she lay in quiet contemplation.

Little Girl was not anxious this time. She went on with her work dili-gently, memorising the features, the landmarks and the energy fields which identified the living creatures that shared the area. Much of this she observed from the trees and during her reconnaissance. She circled the area, checking for signs and scents that would inform her. As she composed a picture of this information, Little Girl began to feel a confidence and sense a freedom. Then, after some days she began to miss Little Boy. The anxiety grew, so, reluctantly, she set off to find him.

She went to T'Ingwe Island – the crossing was easier this time now that the river was diminished, but no more pleasant. She was amazed to see that her brother, who in the new place across the river had grown so suave, was now silly beyond belief. At first she pulled her whiskers forwards in disdain and stiffened her back primly, but something inside her was still alive to the reckless abandon of her own cubhood. She permitted herself to be caught up in the games, reassured. But even in these days there was an awareness that the world had changed. She felt it in her body and she saw it reflected in people's eyes. There was a change in their energies too, an excessive expression of the longing that intrigued her, and as always, the ambiguity of how to respond. It fascinated her, this human way, so different from the detachment she felt. Yet, she had strong feelings for these people who had fed her and protected her and her brother in their cubhood.

The people continued to bring food to the thicket she and her brother had chosen. It was impossible now for them to go back. They needed to keep their distance on the far side of the island. Little Boy submitted himself to the people's ministrations and lay on his back, enjoying the deburring and deticking sessions, but she needed to hold herself apart. Occasionally, she sat close to one of the people, but a hiss would rise involuntarily from her throat if they tried to stroke her. There were times of clarity between her and the people and a mutual understanding flowed from mind to mind. These were the times when she felt most comfortable and was best able to love them in the detached way of leopards.

Soon the restlessness in Little Boy began again. One day, he simply upped and left. He crossed the river without calling for her this time and she didn't see him emerge on the other side. She was tormented by the uncertainty. She wondered if the crocodiles had caught him and paced up and down at the river's edge yowling for him. There was no response. She had never felt so alone.

For a few days, Little Girl remembered staying on the island, growing listless. Then one night while out in the thicket, a lion chased her. It was the closest Little Girl had ever come to death. Up until that point, her natural caution had prevented her from colliding with the mishaps her brother tumbled into. For Little Girl, it was the turning point in the downward spiral her spirit had taken. She heard the lion. It was not difficult – lions were loud, arrogant creatures who made no attempt to conceal themselves. She felt contempt for the way they moved without caution. But she misjudged the lion's proximity. When it came upon her and lunged, his massive paw sweeping through the air with terrifying power, Little Girl somehow managed to shoot up a kigelia tree. She sat there shivering for some time, reprimanding herself for her laxity. She blamed her care-lessness on the lack of concentration that came with her despondent mood. She fell into a sleep state and the answer she sought came to her in a dream. She needed to go back to the new place across the river.

Upon her return she felt stronger, a sense of belonging. She familiarised herself with the changes that had taken place in her absence. She came across the strong scent of lion. Briefly she panicked, thinking her assailant of the previous night was pursuing her. She could tell there were other leopards too; she could feel their presence. The days became alive with new possibilities as she went about her work, identifying landmarks, scenting and scratching posts, reconnaissance points, absorbing all the scents and the sounds. As she worked towards perfect knowledge of the habitat, she began to feel a parallel sense of freedom. There were times when she thought of Little Boy, but the ache she had felt on his parting was gone. Though she felt as bonded to her brother as before, there was no need to find him this time.

Little Girl leapt up the mahogany tree. An elephant cow and her calf were approaching. They moved beneath the branches, silent as thought, majestic in their swaying gait, the youngster in comic imitation of its mother's movement. Little Girl knew of their coming long before they entered the clearing, so finely tuned was she into the energies of this area. She watched them pass and amble down to the river to slurp at the water and then spray it all over themselves.

Little Girl recalled when she first saw an elephant. Little Boy had fall-en clean out of the tree in fright and she had clung so deeply to its bark she could barely unhook her claws, so frightened was she by the enormi-ty of this animal.

The cow and her calf moved further into the water to cool off, the calf squealing, the mother rumbling with maternal contentment as she laid her trunk over his back. Little Girl felt a curious stirring within herself, a sense of unaccustomed pleasure at the maternal scene. She knew the elephant mother was aware of her presence in the branches of the mahogany tree and had chosen to ignore her. After they finished drinking and playing in the water, they returned past the tree. The elephant cow paused momentarily and blew a blast of air through her trunk at the ground, raising the dust around her feet. She was establishing authority and showing her strength. Slowly, the elephant cow turned and raised her huge unblinking eyes at Little Girl. She was astounded at the depth of wisdom carried there. Then with a nod, the mother and her calf ambled off.

The moon edged its way into the sky over Luangwa Valley, its cool light casting shadows from the mahogany tree. Little Girl rearranged herself languidly in the cleft of a branch. Of late, she found herself increasingly drawn to a cluster of stars that had attracted her when they first came to T'Ingwe Island. She lay and stared at the star known at Perseus. Images of the vibrations of light lulled her into a semi-sleep state.

Images of a vast gathering of leopards flowed through her mind. They wanted something from her. What was it they needed to know? It concerned the people. No longer were the images of dreamtime as simple as they had been in her cubhood. Now the images of leopard that came to her were less specific than they had been with the dreams of the mother leopard of Londolozi. There were many leopards now, all leopards, merging and parting with the illogicality of dreams. It was as if she were connected to a vast source.

Little Girl stirred on her branch, her ears swivelling to catch the rustle of leaves as an evening breeze moved through the mahogany. She loved the song of these leaves and the flicker of moonlight and shadow they cast on her body. The dappled effect conspiring with the rosettes of her coat rendered her almost invisible. As her focus shifted inwards and yet further inwards in her meditation, Little Girl felt as if her whole being was becoming lighter and lighter. In the realm into which she was entering, she knew her energies would be restored. This realm was the vibration of all that is and all that has been.